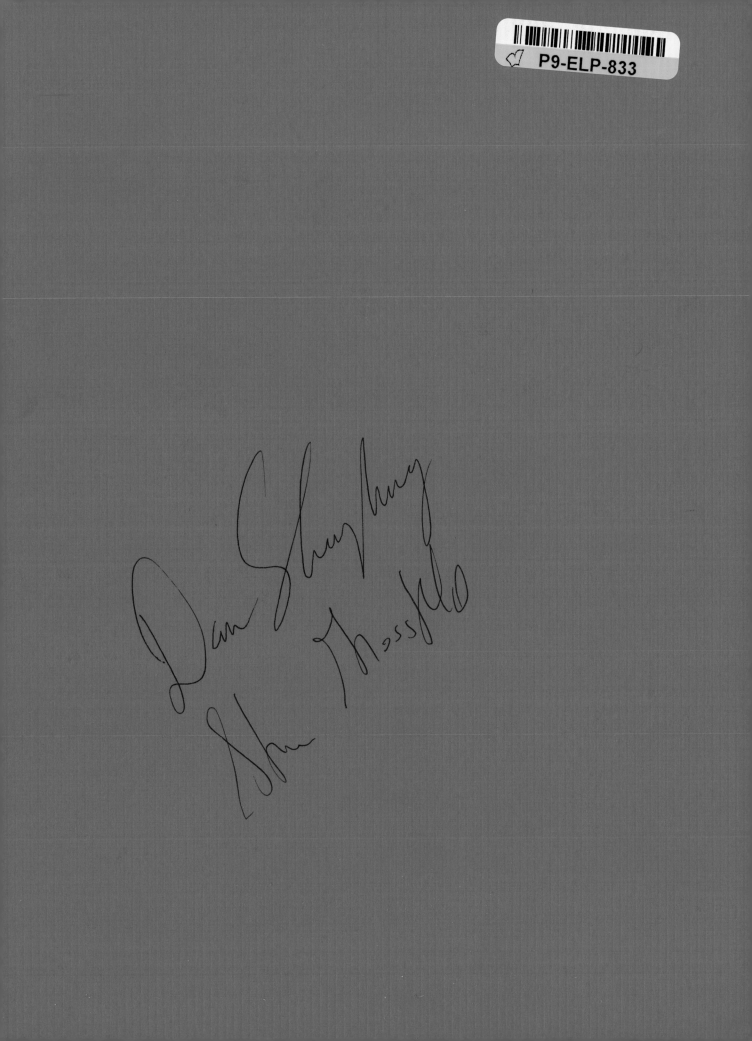

Fenway

That comes back to why the ballparks matter to us — because exac

...omparable people played a comparable game in this ballpark for generation after generation.

— GEORGE WILL

Fenway

A BIOGRAPHY IN WORDS AND PICTURES

DAN SHAUGHNESSY

AND

STAN GROSSFELD

HOUGHTON MIFFLIN COMPANY

BOSTON   NEW YORK   1999

For the two Sams

For information about permission to reproduce
selections from this book, write to
Permissions, Houghton Mifflin Company, 215 Park Avenue
South, New York, New York 10003.

CIP data is available.
ISBN 0-395-94556-9

Printed in the United States of America

WCT 10 9 8 7 6 5 4 3 2 1

PHOTO CREDITS

Boston Globe: pp. 1, 34, 37, 42–43, 47, 111.
Boston Globe / **Stan Grossfeld:** pp. 30, 134, 140.
Boston Globe / **Danny Goshtigian:** p. 112–113.
John F. Kennedy Library: p. 51.
Sports Museum of New England: pp. 20, 38–39, 40, 45.
Leslie Jones, courtesy of Boston Public Library,
    Print Department: pp. 18–19, 22, 29, 32–33, 44, 48.

BOOK DESIGN

Bill Marr, Open Books, LLC, Edgewater, MD

When they raze Fenway,

it'll be like cutting down an old tree.

Count the rings. There's one for each celebration

and heartache suffered by Red Sox fans.

— DAN SHAUGHNESSY

by Ted Williams

When I walked into Fenway Park for the first time in 1939, it certainly looked like a different kind of ballpark. I didn't know if it was good or bad. I knew the right field fence was quite a little ways away. I didn't think it was a hitters' park at all. Right field was 25 feet longer

then than it is now. Center field was always a nice target, which was a great thing for a hitter. Any time you have too short a park in center, you're going to run into a lot of runs and a lot of problems. I don't think I hit my first home run to left field until four years after the first time I played at Fenway. And I told the clubhouse boy I'd never hit another one. He said, "Oh, yes, you will." I never saw many balls hit that way by left-handed hitters who pulled the ball. Charlie Keller could hit them up there. But there weren't as many balls hit long into left field into the screen and now it seems a lot of guys do it. I think that's because of bigger and stronger guys and I think it's because of the ball.

There were no bullpens out there my rookie year, and they thought they had a pretty good young hitter in me. I guess they figured, "We can improve the park and not hurt him any." I think they thought too much of me and then I didn't hit as many home runs my second year. They were pitching me tougher and it was a little harder. Still, I hit .344. But certainly those bullpens were an advantage. They made the ballpark 20 feet shorter.

I played that big right field my first year, but they moved me to left right away. That's an easier part of the ballpark, and they did that for a lot of big hitters. The wall used to be a little different. It was not quite as high and there was a little more of a bank going up to the wall. If you played there all the time, you got accustomed to the ballpark a little bit. I practiced out there, but in those days, the wall partitions weren't as consistent—they were every four feet or so. You'd get a

Three days before his eightieth birthday, Ted Williams demonstrates his hitting technique at his kitchen table in Hernando, Florida.

dead spot and down the ball would go, or you'd get a live spot and it would come back. In some ways, it was a little tougher then because now they come off a little more uniform. I don't remember any balls coming off the ladder. I know we had some funny bounces. You'd go over to back the center fielder up and the damn ball would go into right field. When I played left field, I talked to the guy in the scoreboard. I wanted to know what was going on and what other guys around the league were doing.

I'm glad they're going to change Fenway. I think the park has hurt the game some. I've seen a lot of wonderfully pitched ball games there get screwed up because some little pop fly hits up against that fence. Any time you're helping the hitter or helping the pitcher too much, you're hurting the game. And the thing about this game is that it's been so well balanced with so few changes. Boy, they were lucky to come up with it just like they did.

You are awfully close to the fans at Fenway. I would rather be a little bit farther away from the fans, because when I played I could hear everything. I had rabbit ears. I know the fans like to get close to the field, and there's certain ways you can do it so it doesn't interfere with the game. The fans didn't seem too close when I was in the on-deck circle. All the people who were that close were loyal Red Sox fans. But when I'd go out toward left field I'd get guys out there who weren't so nice.

But center and left field at Fenway are the worst parts about that ballpark. It makes it a little unfair because the greatest advantage to a hitter is when you hit the ball to center. But that's not supposed to be the way it is. It should be the pulled ball that helps the hitter the most. But center and left field in Fenway make it easier because you can wait longer and slap at the ball, which a lot of guys do now, and they get a little cheap hit out there and it takes away from the game. It's only 379 feet to left center. That's kind of close.

Any time you strengthen the pitcher's position more than it should be, or the hitter's position more than it should be, it takes away from the game. Because it's such a balanced game. The pitcher's got to have a reasonable chance in a reasonable ballpark. And so does the hitter. If you don't, you're going to get a low-scoring game in the pitcher's ballpark and a lot of cheap hits in the hitter's ballpark.

Ted, 1939

A lot of guys complained about the background. I never did. I guess the worst situation is when a big left-hander's pitching and the right-handers are looking up into that light in right center. That bothered a lot of guys, but I was used to the ballpark. Plus, there wasn't much foul territory, and that was an advantage for the hitter. But they've enlarged that a little bit since I was there. And I think they tried to keep fans out of that triangle area in center for a while—if they didn't sell out.

I'll tell you what: baseball has not kept pace with some of the improvements that can be made in a ballpark as far as background is concerned. There are three or four new parks that hurt hitters because the backgrounds are bad. Baltimore, when it was first put in, had lights low, and the pitchers threw right out of the lights. And Chicago, when I first went in there, they had a little bitty background. But they've made a lot of improvements, and those are things that have to be improved in the new park in Boston.

But Fenway was like a home to me. It sure was. I was there as long and as often and as much as anybody that I ever knew. I used to go early and get out late. I came in early so I could have some peace and quiet, and if I had to do anything or check anything, I could do it easily. And a lot of mail was delivered to me there. I loved to talk to the trainer and get a lot of my questions answered. I left the park late because I wanted the crowd to disperse.

I can remember the clubhouse. We had little wire seats and little folding chairs. It wasn't as big as it is now, but as long as I was there, they were always improving the park. But they couldn't improve it. Sure, they could make the seats a little better and make this and that a little better—a little bullpen out there—but basically the park has so many nooks and circles and deflections, and that makes it tough.

When I was at Fenway, there was no place under the stands to hit. When I came back to manage with the Senators, they had improved the visitors' club-house because it needed it the most.

When I played in Boston, I never sat at the far end of the dugout. I was always up close, next to the bat rack. I'd have six or eight bats in there and six or eight bats in my locker, and I would try one every now and then. If I thought it was good wood, I'd put it aside, and if anybody wanted a bat of mine, I'd give 'em one of the rejects.

They've been to the World Series in that ballpark. I always thought we had a lot of bad breaks there. When they tear it down, I think it will be a good thing, I really do. Some great pitchers couldn't win in that ballpark. So it'll be a great thing when it happens. Maybe I played so long and played so many games there that I've seen too many great performances get cut in the heart by a bloop hit someplace. Sometimes the configuration of the ballpark just made it unfair.

I love the fans in New England. They're the greatest. They've had some problem years, but they're still hanging in there. All I can tell you about Boston is that the fans cannot be beat. And I hope they win a World Series. I don't want to live to be a helluva lot older than I am, but I want to tell you something. Someday, I would like to look in the stars and say, "Damn, we did it."

All in all, Fenway's been a historic, absolutely unique place. It's one of the oldest ballparks, and I certainly have a love and affection for it because it has a ton of memories. Still, I can't wait until I see the new park when it's done. I want Boston to have the best. If any city needed a new ballpark, they need it. I won't shed a tear. Take a lot of good pictures of it.

Hernando, Florida
August 1998

We love baseball

because it seizes and retains the past,

like the snowy village inside a glass paperweight.

— DONALD HALL

Dan Shaughnessy, 1968

by Dan Shaughnessy

It's personal.

There's no other way to explain the sentimental feelings many of us have for old, inanimate objects like sweaters, cars, houses, and baseball parks. I still have the maroon wool cardigan that my coach, John Fahey, gave me in 1969 (the year Tony C. staged

his dramatic comeback) when I lettered in baseball as a sophomore at Groton High School. The sweater has a big "G" on the right side, and for more than two years I got to walk the corridors of GHS feeling cool. I haven't worn that sweater since the early '70s, but I could never throw it away.

Then there's the 1987 maroon Volvo 240 DL station wagon in my driveway. We brought my youngest child, Sam, home from the hospital in this car on October 4, 1987 (the day Roger Clemens won his twentieth to clinch his second straight Cy Young trophy), and I fully expect Sam to be driving the same clunky wagon to his Newton North High School games in the next century.

The house in which I grew up was built early in this century, and my folks owned it from 1946 (when the Red Sox played the Cardinals in the World Series) until my mom sold it in the spring of 1988 (the year of Joe Morgan Magic at Fenway). On the last night, three of my siblings, my mom, and I sat in folding chairs around a card table in the empty living room and ate Chinese take-out. We told growing-up stories for the last time in the drafty old Victorian, then said good-bye. It was teary, and I remember it as the only time my brother ever hugged me. It's been more than ten years since that night, and my oldest sister, now in her fifties, drives past the house on a regular

basis yet still cannot bear to look.

That's probably what I'll do when the Red Sox tear down Fenway Park.

It's personal.

Cynics are having a field day with folks like myself. I think it All-Started with Donald Hall's wonderful "Fathers Playing Catch with Sons" (1985). The baseball-as-life metaphor has become a droopy cliché, and ever since Ken Burns carpet-bombed us with eighteen hours of baseball history and folklore in 1994—complete with endless head shots of literati waxing poetic on the sport—it has been fashionable to bash those who hold baseball close to their heart.

So bash away. I won't be one of those thousands of Save Fenway zealots, hugging the brick walls and lying down in front of bulldozers, but before Fenway is gone I plan to spend some time in the empty yard, remembering all the things that happened there and contemplating what it has meant to my life. When they raze Fenway, it'll be like cutting down an old tree. Count the rings. There's one for each celebration and heartache suffered by Red Sox fans.

Tiger Stadium is officially terminal. The new Detroit ballyard opens in 2000, and when that happens Fenway can claim to have been the home of major league baseball longer than any ballpark in the history of the planet. This is no small achievement.

The Red Sox first started playing big league ball in Fenway on April 20, 1912, just a few days after the White Star liner *Titanic* sank to the bottom of the North Atlantic. The collective memory of Red Sox Nation no longer goes back to the days before Fenway. As it awaits the wrecking ball, probably sometime early in the new century, Fenway stands as the only place any of us remember the Red Sox playing home games. And so many of those memories are merged with our own life passages.

More than any sport, baseball is about generations. Watching a baseball game, parents and kids have time to talk with one another. There is plenty of time between pitches and between innings, and although the days of fifty-cent bleacher seats are long gone, going to Fenway is still considerably cheaper than attending a pro football, basketball, or hockey game. Meanwhile, the major league marketing czars haven't yet bombarded us with rock music between pitches (though it's probably coming), and this rare silence, coupled with the pace of the game, allows for conversation and even storytelling in the stands. This makes baseball unique. Try making conversation during a Magic–Lakers game amid the din of the O-Rena in downtown, yahoo Orlando.

Most of us, later in life, remember going to baseball games with Dad and Mom. And as parents, we cherish the first visits to Fenway with our own children. I've yet to meet a New England Patriots fan who remembers his first visit with Dad to Foxborough—the aluminum-seat-filled Levittown of American stadia. Quite simply, none of the other three major sports offers family fun the way baseball does. The other games are too expensive, too loud, and—in the case of all football and some hockey games—too rowdy.

Apart from my childhood home and the one where I now live, Fenway Park is just about my favorite place on Earth. Some folks would name Disneyland, Walden Pond, Yellowstone, or a sweet summer spot on old Cape Cod. Good for them. For me, it's an endangered baseball park that'll soon celebrate its ninetieth birthday.

My father took me to Fenway for the first time in 1961, Yaz's rookie season, when I was eight years old. It was a night game against the Orioles and the Red Sox won. Later that season, I had an offer to go to Fenway for a doubleheader against the Tigers. It would be a long day, I was warned, and they didn't want any complaining or whining about leaving early. No problem. Sitting in the right field grandstand, I watched Al Kaline's back (he was number 6) for 18 innings.

For ten years I had to go into Boston once a year for asthma checkups at the old Lahey Clinic on Commonwealth Avenue. The reward was a Sox game at Fenway. It also taught me a lot about disappointment. There was nothing worse than rain on the day of our trip to Boston. Even now, unexpected disappointment reminds me of a Red Sox rainout on the day I went to Boston when I was twelve years old. On the brighter side, I still remember being fifteen and seeing Denny McLain win one of his 31 games in the summer of 1968. We sat in section 1 in right field. The worst seats in the house. Who cared? It was a part of baseball history—like getting to see Mark McGwire hit a home run in the summer of 1998.

When I finally got my driver's license, my friends and I would motor from Groton to the Riverside T lot on Route 128 in Newton. We'd hop on the Green Line inbound to the Fenway Park stop, then walk with the rest of the Sox legions to our hardball Mecca. Perfect. That way, we got to see night games at Fenway without having to drive in Boston. During those same years, I remember taking a school field trip to Boston for a Saturday game with the Oakland A's. The A's scored a million runs, and Reggie Jackson knocked home about ten with a flat-sided bat that was later ruled illegal. When I was a high school senior, I drove into Boston for a day game and invited a hometown girl who was studying at Simmons (conveniently located two blocks from Fenway). We sat in the bleachers and had to move every couple innings so she could maximize the sun's exposure on her face.

As a sophomore at Holy Cross, I went to Fenway with a bunch of fellow Crusaders in 1973 to see the Yankees and Red Sox. We saw Ron Blomberg and Orlando Cepeda make history as baseball's first designated hitters. During my college summers I was a legislative intern, and in those days the state representatives had Fenway passes, which enabled them to gain admission for fifty cents. My state

Opening Day, 1956

rep gave me his pass, and I spent many a weekday after-noon studying John Curtis and Rogelio Moret at the tax-payers' expense. It was there that I met a man, now a Massachusetts Superior Court judge, who told me that he used to grade bar exams sitting in the stands at Fenway. It still tickles me to think that there are lawyers in this state who possibly passed the bar because my friend was happy about a Jim Rice grand slam.

It wasn't until 1975 that I first walked into Fenway in any professional capacity. Standing on the field and in the dugout and seeing the clubhouses for the first time, I felt a new love for the old place. I wasn't going to play for the Red Sox, but I would begin my career in the old green ballyard where I'd spent so many days and nights with my family and friends.

As a quote runner for the Associated Press legend Dave O'Hara, I made seven dollars per game at Fenway in the summer of '75. It was probably the best job I ever had. Along with my best pal, Kevin Dupont, I got to eat dinner every night in the pressroom before games, then hang around and listen to the old-timers talk baseball long after the Red Sox had won or lost. It was in the old wooden

Fenway pressroom that I introduced myself to Tom Yawkey, the owner of the Red Sox, who looked like the custodian, and had dinner with Jumpin' Joe Dugan, who had been Babe Ruth's roommate while playing third base for the 1927 New York Yankees. Dugan told me that I ate more than Ruth; probably I did. After all, the food was free, and I was in debt because of college loans. There were nights when Billy Martin waxed crude. Eyes wide, I listened to Dick O'Connell, Calvin Griffith, and Earl Weaver. I got to drink with the gods and soak up their stories and their hardball wisdom.

My status as an AP quote runner enabled me to buy tickets to the 1975 World Series at Fenway, so I was with my sister Ann in section 27 when Carlton Fisk clanged his home run for the ages in Game 6.

Section 27 is also where I saw my father for the last time, in September of 1979. We shared a handshake in the stands before I went to work, covering the Baltimore Orioles in the visitors' clubhouse. My dad died a month later, while I was covering the World Series in Baltimore. He was buried next to a Little League ball field in Pepperell, Massachusetts.

The demolition of the Boston Garden, 1998

Each of my three children was born during baseball season, at Boston's Beth Israel Hospital, where some rooms have a view of Fenway Park. A few hours after my daughter, Kate, was born on July 30, 1985, I walked down to Fenway and handed out cigars to the writers behind the batting cage covering the Red Sox night game against the White Sox.

More than a decade later, I bring the kids to Fenway regularly. They complain about our crappy old cars, but never about the inconveniences of the ancient ballpark. We don't mind standing every time the guy in the middle of our row has to go out to get another beer. We don't mind the poles that occasionally obscure Nomar at short or Pedro on the mound. I take some weird comfort in the knowledge that these poles are the same green beams that blocked the vision of my dad and his dad when they would take the trolley in from Cambridge to watch the Red Sox in the 1920s.

The old Boston Garden served as New England's indoor sports palace from 1928 to 1995 and came to be part of the identity of the Boston Bruins and Celtics. With small seats, obstructed views, smelly bathrooms, pitiful parking, zero air conditioning, tiny concessions, and loud fans who sat practically on top of the team benches, everything about the Garden was Boston. On television, in person, or even on the radio (the Garden had a distinct horn to signify the end of a period or quarter), you knew where the game was being played.

In the name of progress, air conditioning, and luxury boxes, the Garden went dark in the fall of 1995 and yielded to a generic arena built less than a foot from the old building and named after a bank. The FleetCenter has proven to be clean, expensive, air-conditioned, and completely soulless. Fans no longer have obstructed views, but they are so far back from the court or ice, they can barely make out the players' numbers. Forty-seven percent of the seats in the new Garden would fall outside the physical confines of the old building. The top row of the old Garden was 105 feet from center court. The top row of the new building is 164 feet from the same spot. The distant fans certainly can't be heard. Appropriately enough, watching a game at the FleetCenter is like watching a game in a bank. The bathrooms and concession stands are pristine and plentiful, and escalators and elevators assist fans in search of comfort, but there is nothing Boston about the place. The Bruins and Celtics have lost their home advantage. There is nothing memorable about the experience.

Because of the FleetCenter, concert promoters in Boston can now compete with the likes of Hartford, Springfield, Worcester, and Providence. Big deal. Elton John and Billy Joel no longer fear the acoustics of Boston's big arena, but the Montreal Canadiens and Los Angeles Lakers aren't afraid of the new building either. That's where Boston lost. The Garden had the ghosts and the glory, along with the heart and soul of our teams and our town.

The Garden was also relatively affordable compared to the new joint. And that's something else we'll lose when the Red Sox move from Fenway to a new home. *Boston Magazine* called Fenway "the best-loved symbol of Boston's egalitarianism." The next ballyard will no doubt squeeze low-end ticket buyers out of the market. As great as Camden Yards and Jacobs Field are, the everyday people no longer go to games in Baltimore and Cleveland. One of the beauties of big city baseball has been its availability. College kids in their dorms should be able to hear the beginning of a game on the radio, then hike over to the yard and watch the finish from the cheap seats. It's always been that way with Fenway. Not much longer.

Webb Nichols, an architect in Watertown, wrote in the *Globe*, "As a place of public assembly, a stadium or ballpark is an expression of the involvement of a community in the life and passion of the time. However, it is the game through which we bear our collective witness as a community. It is only the game that creates a common memory binding those who were there together. It is the experience of the game that is under assault."

But there is no going back, no hope for those who would preserve Fenway. The tide shifted irreversibly when Camden Yards was opened in 1992. The baseball commissioner, Bud Selig, said in 1998, "Camden Yards may have been the single most important change in the economics of sports."

In 1987 the Red Sox commissioned an engineering report, which predicted twenty more years of structural safety at Fenway, but only if the club followed a detailed and expensive maintenance and repair program. The Sox presently spend more than $1 million annually on maintenance, and when a 500-pound beam fell in Yankee Stadium in the spring of 1998, there were more calls for the end of Fenway.

Much as I hate to admit it, Fenway simply doesn't work anymore. This hard truth became painfully apparent to me in the summer of 1998, when I was under the stands during the third inning of a Red Sox–Phillies game. The ballpark was sold out and the stands appeared full, yet the underbelly of Fenway was crammed with thousands of hot, sweaty people standing in line for every possible concession and convenience. There was a long line for the ATM machines, long lines for beer, and long lines for the bathrooms. It occurred to me that a Sox ticket holder could spend twenty minutes in line for cash, another twenty queuing up for beer, then a final five minutes waiting to use the men's room. That's three-quarters of an hour off the clock, just for a beer.

The amazing part about all of the above is that Sox fans don't complain. They have been conditioned to settle for less in the name of nostalgia, and many have never experienced any other major league park. But Sox fans who've traveled to Baltimore, Cleveland, and Anaheim know that it doesn't have to be this way. Like Red Sox executives, they agree that a new park will allow the team to remain fiscally competitive in the American League East while offering Boston fans the same amenities that

Fenway preservationists state their case.

fans in other cities consider routine.

In the name of fiscal competitiveness, old sports palaces must be replaced by new ones with luxury boxes, food courts, and fan amenities. So we want to preserve Fenway in words and pictures, in a book. It is our tribute to a place that's been part of our lives, a place that appears doomed.

In 1998, Rick Reilly wrote in *Sports Illustrated*, "Let me get this straight: We're bulldozing real vintage ballparks like Tiger Stadium and Fenway Park to put up fake vintage ballparks?" Sadly, this appears to be the case.

Stan Grossfeld, the eyes of this book, grew up in the Bronx and got to watch the Mick in center field, beating the tar out of the Red Sox year after year when we were kids in the 1950s and '60s. Stan is a baseball guy. I have never seen him happier than when he personally thanked Fay Vincent, then commissioner, for suspending George Steinbrenner from baseball. Fortunately for those of us who love Fenway, Stan is now a card-carrying citizen of Red Sox Nation, and his affection for our park comes across in his photographs here.

When I talked to Ted Williams about shedding a tear for old Fenway, he shrugged off the suggestion and told me, "Take a lot of good pictures of it."

So that's what Stan went out and did. And this is our book about it. And it's personal.

Nantucket, September 1998

The mayor of Boston, John "Honey Fitz" Fitzgerald, tosses out the first ball before a World Series game in Fenway's inaugural season of 1912. His daughter, young Rose Fitzgerald (later Mrs. Joseph P. Kennedy), is at far right.

Previous page: Fenway, 1912

A religious shrine or a giant pinball machine? The House of Usher or a house of pain? Museum or amusement park? Historical or hysterical? The oldest park in the major leagues, the last of the single-deck baseball theaters, Fenway Park has inspired more lavish praise and outrageous comparison than any American sports arena. New York's House That Ruth Built is certainly the ballpark most steeped in honor and history, but nobody ever compared Yankee Stadium to the Sistene Chapel. Perhaps Fenway is showered with torrents of purple prose because the park is in New England, the home of more poets, bards, pop psychologists, and writers than any American pocket.

The estimable John Updike dubbed it a "lyric little bandbox" and wrote that Fenway represents "a compromise between Man's Euclidean determinations and Nature's beguiling irregularities." The late, great House Speaker Tip O'Neill (born in 1912, the same year as Fenway) said, "It's like being in an English theatre. You're right on top of the stage. So chummy." Bill Lee called it "a shrine where people come for religious rites." The former Yankee manager Buck Showalter said, "I don't know anything about classical music, but if there's a baseball symphony, this is it." And to think that Mo Vaughn, the former Sox star, said, "Blow the damn place up."

Blow it up? That's precisely what happened in Cincinnati, Philadelphia, and Pittsburgh in the 1960s: Cincinnati's Crosley Field gave way to Riverfront Stadium. Philadelphia lost Connie Mack Stadium and got the Vet. Pittsburgh's charming Forbes Field was demolished and replaced by another spaceship cookie-cutter called Three Rivers Stadium. It seemed like progress at the time, but now fans in all three cities long for the good old days and the good old ballparks. In the summer of '98, the Pirates announced plans to build a $228-million ballpark that'll remind fans of old Forbes Field. Everything old is new again—only more expensive.

THE RED SOX DID NOT ALWAYS PLAY THEIR HOME GAMES at Fenway Park. Boston's charter American League franchise was formed in 1901, and the Huntington Grounds served quite nicely for the first eleven years of its history. Less than a mile from Fenway, at the corner of Huntington and Rogers avenues, the wood stadium was the site of the first World Series—won by the Red Sox (actually, they were the Pilgrims then) over the Pittsburgh Pirates in September 1903. Happily, the park was just a short walk from the watering hole of the immortal 'Nuff Ced McGreevey. 'Nuff Ced's bar was called Third Base because that's your last stop on the way home, and there fans gathered before and after games to drink and discuss baseball. Today the site of the Huntington Grounds is part of the campus of Northeastern University, and the only baseball memento is a statue of Cy Young and a plaque dedicated in 1993. The area certainly looks nothing like it did after the turn of the twentieth century, when it was owned by the New York, New Haven, and Hartford Railroad. There's no railyard soot gathering on the cap of the Cy Young statue.

That first park was built in less than two months in the spring of 1901, and the Pilgrims drew 289,448 in their inaugural season in the renegade American League. They finished first in 1903 and '04 and led the league in attendance with a whopping 623,295 (not including thousands of daily gate-crashers) in 1904.

In 1910 John I. Taylor, the owner of the Red Sox (a perk given to him by his dad, who owned the *Boston Globe*), decided not to renew his lease at the Huntington Grounds. The Taylor family was intent on selling the club and knew it could seek a higher price, and attract more bidders, if a ballpark was part of the deal. On June 24, 1911, Taylor announced his intention to build a new park for the Boston Red Sox (Taylor had snatched the new name when the crosstown Boston Nationals abandoned their carmine hose in favor of white stockings in 1907).

The *Boston Globe*, not surprisingly, provided exhaustive coverage for the announcement. It ran a half-page sketch of the proposed park and an accompanying story that concluded: "With the new park covering 365,306 square feet of land and the stands of the most approved type, and the home club brought up to its best pitch, the fans hereabouts can confidently look forward through the winter months to some great baseball games next season."

The plot of land for the new ballpark was in the Fenway area, between Lansdowne and Jersey streets. New trolley lines served the area and made it an appealing site for the Taylors. The Fenway had been a smelly mudflat until 1881–85, when it was drained as part of a plan to include it in the Emerald Necklace envisioned by Frederick Law Olmsted, the noted landscape architect. The area was Boston's last filled-in district, but the plan to make it part of the necklace was eventually scrapped.

Like the Red Sox and the *Globe,* the land for the new park was already owned by the Taylors; more specifically, by the Fenway Realty Company, another Taylor holding company. Taylor had purchased the land after buying the Red Sox in 1904. Part of Boston folklore is John I. Taylor's alleged reason for naming the field. His famous quote

goes: "It's in the Fenway, isn't it? Then call it Fenway Park." That sounds nice, but in fact the name was intended to promote Fenway Realty.

This brings up a cruel joke. In the next five to ten years, the successor to Fenway Park will no doubt have some commercial name attached to it, and diehard Red Sox fans will be mortified and stupefied at the thought of paying homage to Gillette Field or Reebok Yards. This is what happened when a major Providence bank, Fleet, put its name on the building that replaced the Boston Garden. Some sports fans still have difficulty saying "FleetCenter." It's the New Garden.

Today, almost every modern sports palace (such as Coors Field, Pro Player Park, United Center, and Qualcomm) sells its name to the highest corporate bidder. The Pirates got $42 million from PNC Bank Corp. for the right to name their new stadium. The Red Sox no doubt will do the same thing. And when this happens, New England purists would do well to remember that Wrigley Field is named after chewing gum, and Fenway Park amounted to free publicity for the Taylors' realty company. If Boston's next baseball facility is named Century 21 Park, it would only be consistent with the Taylors' action in 1912.

Fenway Park was a land deal, nothing more. When construction was under way, the Taylors sold half their interest in the Red Sox for a reported $150,000, covering their original investment. They also retained ownership of the park. Sweet deal.

Before the ballpark was built, a church and the Park Riding School were the area's most visible structures. There was no Citgo sign, no Green Monster, no Pizzeria Uno in Kenmore Square.

The Red Sox broke ground on September 25, 1911, for one of the first steel and concrete parks in the world. The first known baseball park was the Brooklyn Grounds, built in 1862. The enclosed diamond had special benches for ladies and another section for gamblers. The outfield fences were 500 feet from home plate and, like every other park built before Fenway, it was made predominantly of wood. In an age when almost all the fans smoked, wood stadiums routinely caught fire. Ironically, although Fenway was built with considerable fireproof material, it

The 1912 World Champion Red Sox. The team won 105 games during the season and beat the New York Giants in the World Series.

would twice be damaged by fire before 1935.

Fenway was built by the Charles Logue Building Company; James E. McLaughlin was the chief architect, and the Osborn Engineering Company of Cleveland provided civil engineering services. Erected on 365,308 square feet of urban space, Fenway cost $650,000 to build, which was accomplished totally with private funding—no mention of personal seat licenses, luxury boxes, or state funding for infrastructure. Upon completion, the park was assessed at $420,000 (now the average sale price of a home in Newton), the land at $344,000.

John I. Logue, a grandson of the man who built Fenway, wrote in 1995: "It's important to me and my extended family that my grandfather is known as the builder of the ballpark which is so prominent in the history of baseball. In the family records, we have a picture of Charles Logue with John Taylor, the Red Sox owner, and the Comiskey brothers, visiting from Chicago, at the Opening Day luncheon. However, the game was rained out."

In the intervening years there have been hundreds of changes, including obvious ones like light towers, bullpens, the giant video screen, the 600 Club (rising behind home plate like a monster aquarium filled with rich fish), elevators, luxury suites, and an ATM machine under the first base grandstand. There was certainly no Legal Sea Food clam chowder on sale for four dollars in 1912, and it's doubtful that Tris Speaker called his agent from a cell phone in the home team's clubhouse. Even Jersey Street has been renamed (it's now Yawkey Way). But if you stand there and gaze up at the red brick of Fenway's main entrance, you are looking at the same facade that greeted fans attending the first exhibition game, between the Red Sox and Harvard, on April 9, 1912. The front of Fenway, patterned after Philadelphia's Shibe Park, is designed in a tapestried red brick Boston Colonial style, replete with diamond patterns, mosaics, and keystone arches. Like the main entrance to the Fairmont Copley Plaza Hotel, also built in 1912, the front of Fenway is frozen in time. It could be used to shoot a scene from *The Fitzgeralds and the Kennedys* and hold up quite well.

Much of the asymmetry that has made Fenway so charming and diabolical through the years can be attrib-

The Royal Rooters, a band of everyday Sox fans, riot in 1912 v

uted to Boston's crazy maze of streets and rail lines. Anyone who has driven in the Hub knows that the street pattern makes no sense, and Fenway's dimensions are directly related to this nightmare.

One doesn't need aerial photography to conclude that Boston has no standard grid design. Legend has it that many of the roads started out as cowpaths, which helps explain the city's geographic smorgasbord. Fenway Park is framed by Brookline Avenue, Yawkey Way, Lansdowne Street, Ipswich Street, and Van Ness Street. This beast is no Pentagon, however, although the self-

...ir seats are sold to other customers before the next-to-last game of the World Series.

importance of the Red Sox front office might lead one to believe otherwise. It was Mo Vaughn who, in the spring of 1998, referred to John Harrington and Dan Duquette, CEO and general manager of the Sox respectively, as "the Joint Chiefs of Staff."

Even with its relatively small footprint, Fenway could have been symmetrical, but concessions to the street layout had to be made once the Taylor family called for team offices on the Jersey Street side. There was no thought of night baseball in 1911, so the architects had to make sure batters would not be facing into the sun late in the after-noon. Thus home plate was set in the southwest corner of the yard (magnetic north is just a few degrees to the right of the left field line) to ensure that the sun would set behind third base, bothering only the right fielder. This meant that Lansdowne Street would be only a little more than 300 feet from home plate, so there would be no seating beyond the left field fence. Lansdowne Street was banked on its far side by the Boston & Albany Railroad. Since the Sox couldn't move outward, they eventually moved up (the skyscraper syndrome), and so the Green Monster was born. More on that later. Much more.

Fenway Park was first used for football by the Boston Redskins in the 1930s.

The placement of the outfield fences was not a big issue in 1912. It was the deadball era, and players were not hitting the ball 350 feet. The fences were supposed to eliminate gate-crashing and free looks from the street. Today, league rules govern field dimensions (the fences in new parks must be at least 325 feet from home plate), but one of the beauties of baseball parks is that each one has its own dimensions. Football and basketball share none of this—fields and courts are "regulation." Hockey had some unique rinks through the years (the Boston Garden had a notoriously small ice surface and the Bruins built their teams accordingly), but baseball was the sport with fields like snowflakes—no two were alike. Thanks in part to its fences, Boston's park is an architectural mutant.

Fenway was not quite complete when the Red Sox beat Harvard, 2–0, in its first exhibition game. Sod had been transplanted from the Huntington Grounds, but there were no right field bleachers yet and only a small section of seats in center. The area beyond right field was roped off for parking. (The rest of the bleachers were not added until the Sox made it to the 1912 World Series.) The event did not attract the 10,000 men of Harvard. Only 3,000 fans attended the weather-shortened (snow flurries in April) exhibition game against the Johnnies.

The park's first American League game, against the New York Highlanders, was scheduled for April 18, but rain pushed it back to Saturday, April 20. By that time not as many people cared. The *Titanic* had gone down on April 15, and the Cunard liner *Carpathia* arrived in New York with survivors the day before the game. Naturally, there was little talk of baseball, as newspapers scrambled for any and all information about the disaster. The day after Fenway opened, it got two paragraphs on the front page of the *Boston Globe*. The headline SOX OPEN TO PACKED PARK was dwarfed by THRICE WARNED, a survivor's chilling account of three iceberg warnings that were allegedly transmitted from the crow's nest of the *Titanic* to the officer on the steamship's bridge.

The Red Sox won the opener, beating New York, 7–6, in 11 innings. Admission was twenty-five cents for the bleachers, fifty cents for the pavilion. Tris Speaker knocked home the winning run. Throwing out the first ball was Boston's mayor, John "Honey Fitz" Fitzgerald. Again, Fenway was awash in history—past, present, and future. Not only was the ballpark dedicated in the same week the *Titanic* sank, but the first pitch was hurled by the grandfather-to-be of John F. Kennedy. Our thirty-fifth president was not born until five years later.

Fenway Park had the first electric scoreboard, a curious feature in 1912, and 18 turnstiles, more than any ballpark in the majors. Fans could get there easily: it was a short walk from Kenmore Square and near the Ipswich Street trolley line. There were some complaints about the bleachers being too far from the action, but the park was well received in most initial reports.

In the early years, the Red Sox almost could not lose at their new home field. The 1912 Red Sox edition (still known as "the Speed Boys" in many accounts), went 57–20 at home and beat the New York Giants in 7 games to win the World Series. They hit only 29 homers, however, 6 fewer than they hit a year earlier at the Huntington Grounds. Two years later, the National League Boston Braves borrowed Fenway for the World Series and beat the Philadelphia A's in four straight. The Sox won World Series again in 1915, 1916 (though these were played at the new Braves Field, which was larger), and 1918. Yankee Stadium still hadn't been built, but it certainly seemed as though Fenway was going to be the home of champions for a long time. When Babe Ruth hurled Boston to a Series victory over the Cubs in 6 games in 1918, the park was only seven years old but had already been the home of four championship teams and had served as the World Series site for another. Who knew that that was probably going to be it for the remainder of the century?

Meanwhile, the ballpark had an impact on the city.

The site was originally considered part of Boston's perimeter, but the neighborhood expanded in the early years of the park to become a prime residential and commercial district. Fenway Park was the catalyst for this urban development, like an early Camden Yards or Jacobs Field.

Today, baseball purists are horrified by the sacrilegious giant Coke bottles on the left field light tower, but there is plenty of tacky precedent. Early pictures of Fenway show a much smaller left field wall plastered with advertisements for whiskey, razor blades, and soap.

Fenway was the third-largest park in the country when it opened, but there were still some overflow crowds; when this happened, the management simply put ropes in the outfield and let the fans sit behind the Sox outfielders. The 10-foot-high sloped area in front of the left field wall (named Duffy's Cliff because of the talent of the Sox left fielder Duffy Lewis) was especially popular because it afforded the best view. Putting fans behind the rope called for some interesting ground rules, but none like the ones laid down after the first Fenway fire, in 1926. The May blaze wiped out the bleachers along the left field foul line; the section was not repaired for almost a decade.

The sale of Babe Ruth to the Yankees in the winter of 1919–20 has been well documented, and Boston's baseball fans still lament the deal, blaming eighty years of subsequent bad luck on the Curse of the Bambino. It's a nifty, superstition-over-science theme and conveniently explains eight decades of disappointment and near misses, but it's often forgotten that the beloved Boston ballpark was also part of the deal. Sad but true. Harry Frazee, the owner of the Sox, sent Ruth to Jacob Ruppert, the Yankees' owner, for $125,000 and a $350,000 loan for a mortgage on Fenway. So not only did the Sox lose the greatest player in baseball history, but their home field was owned by the hated Yankees until 1933, when a thirty-year-old millionaire, Thomas A. Yawkey, bought the team from Bob Quinn, the owner since 1926. It's no wonder that the Red Sox kept sending good players to New York after Ruth was sold. The Yankees' owner was Boston's landlord, and dear Fenway was Frazee's hardball collateral. When Yawkey bought the team, he asked Ruppert to carry the note for another year, but everything

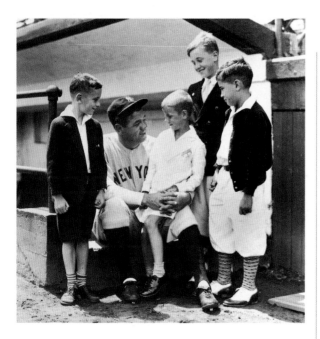

The Babe — a member of the Red Sox from 1914 to 1919 — visits with kids on his return as a Yankee.

Previous page: Well-dressed vendors hawk cigarettes outside Fenway Park during World War I.

changed when the Red Sox beat the Yanks five straight times in 1933. Ruppert demanded full payment and Yawkey cut him a check at once, restoring the independence and dignity of Fenway Park.

Yawkey's next move was to renovate the park. At the end of the 1933 season, the young Boston owner sank more than a million Depression dollars into the rebuilding. There was a discouraging setback after New Year's Day when Boston's worst fire in twelve years beset Fenway. Yawkey's response was to replace the wooden stands in center field with concrete bleachers. He also ripped out the wooden seats in left and right field, extended the bleachers to the left field wall, built new seating in right field, added 6,000 grandstand seats, and built the press box, which lasted until 1989. In all, 15,708 new seats were installed to make Fenway's official capacity 37,500, the sixth largest in baseball. Yawkey even had workers sandblast the Jersey Street entrance. Fenway sparkled again.

Yawkey's home renovation also gave birth to the single most important element of Fenway Park, the Green Monster. Duffy's Cliff was dug up and replaced by a 37-foot-high fence of sheet metal and steel. Two years later a 23-foot-high screen—designed to save baseballs and protect windows on Lansdowne Street—was added to the top of the fence.

It is impossible to overstate what the Wall means to Fenway. It has changed the way the Red Sox play baseball, sometimes saving them, but more often killing them (hello, Bucky Dent). It would be difficult to find another sports arena with a feature as famous as Fenway's Green Monster. Yankee Stadium has monument park and one portion of the famous upper-deck facade, but neither compares with Fenway's Monster.

The Red Sox are committed either to taking the Wall with them to their next park or building something similar and preserving the Green Monster in a baseball museum. New York's owner George Steinbrenner faced the same dilemma when he rebuilt Yankee Stadium in 1973. The upper-deck facade was the park's signature fixture, but because of its weight, it was impossible to make it part of the renovated park (which has no poles).

"In 1970, the facade went all around the stadium," remembered Steinbrenner. "In 1973, I was sitting with a dear friend of mine, who has now passed—Terry Grant. He was a great baseball fan. We were pals and we'd sit in those old boxes and they were going to redo the whole stadium. He asked what we were going to do with the facade that made the stadium familiar to everybody. I didn't know and I called the engineer and he said we had no plans for it. Terry was an artistic guy and he told me that the beauty of that could not be lost. The new overhangs wouldn't take the weight, so we put some piece of it in center field and it's still there today."

Wrigley Field's ivy outfield walls probably come closest to matching Fenway's Monster monument. And Chicago's buildings across Waveland Avenue beyond Wrigley's left field fence might be compared with Boston's towering Citgo sign—which has inspired at least one song and a three-minute movie. The sign looms over the Green Monster and serves as an unofficial Boston monument, not unlike the eyes of Dr. Eckelberg in F. Scott Fitzgerald's *Great Gatsby.* The Citgo sign was built in 1965 and went dark during the energy crisis of the late 1970s, but it was rescued when sentimental citizens petitioned the Boston

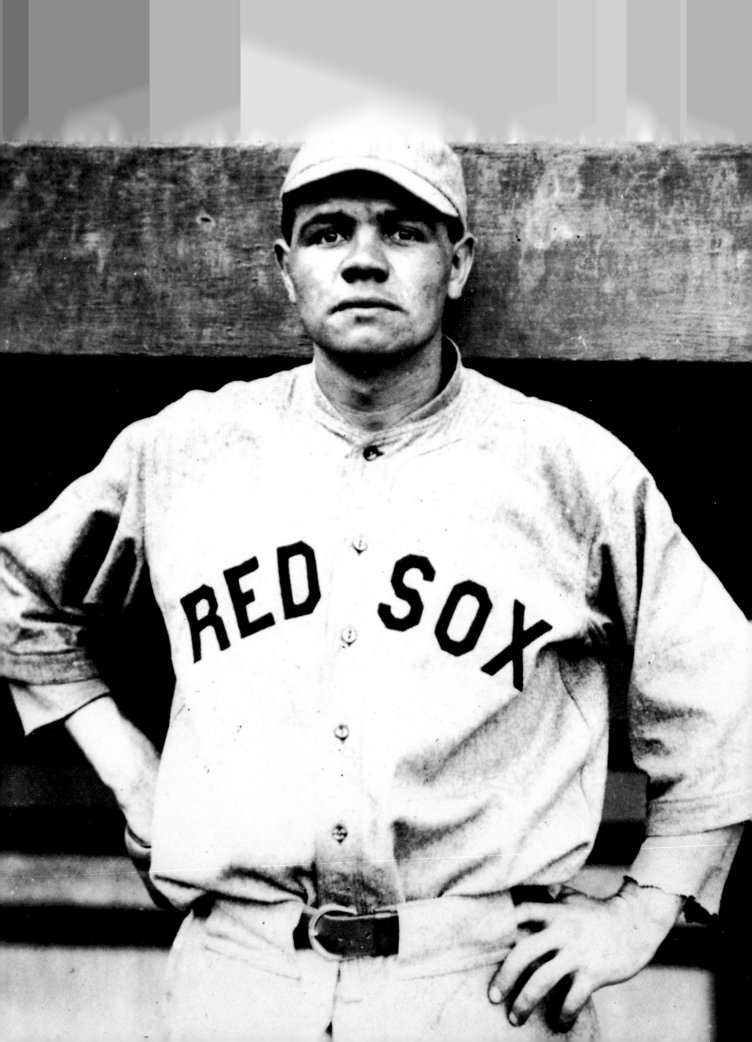

Landmarks Commission. Renovated in 1983, it serves as an ever-present distant cousin to the Green Monster.

With the Wall in place and the rest of the park fully renovated (losing more foul territory behind home plate), Yawkey gave Boston fans in 1934 the park we know today. In 1999, some seats in Fenway provide a view virtually identical to the one you would have had in the summer of 1934. The poet Donald Hall wrote: "We love baseball because it seizes and retains the past, like the snowy village inside a glass paperweight." That is what Fenway does for us as it prepares to usher in another century of major league baseball in Boston.

The bullpens were added in 1940, after Ted Williams's rookie season. The pens gave the relief pitchers a sanctuary from the sidelines and moved the right field fences 23 feet closer to home plate. Oddly enough, Williams's homer total went from 31 to 23 the year after the bullpens were installed, but Teddy Ballgame and every lefty who came after him eventually took advantage of the cozier dimensions.

The bullpens are fan favorites. Right field is where young fans have a chance to engage in conversation with pitchers and catchers from both teams. Bill Lee always had a lot of fun with the bleacher creatures, and Bob Stanley delighted the masses by smashing beachballs with a bullpen rake. Dennis Eckersley, who first came to Fenway in 1975 and returned to the Red Sox in '98, still speaks of "smelling weed" from his perch in the bullpen. The Oriole pitcher Ross Grimsley was involved in one of the more controversial bullpen moments when he fired a ball at a heckling fan in the 1970s. Trying to scare the fan, he threw the ball at a protective screen, but the baseball somehow penetrated the screen, struck the fan, and provoked a lawsuit.

In 1963, Cleveland's right fielder Al Luplow made what is considered the greatest catch in Fenway history when he took a home run away from the Sox's pinch-hitter Dick Williams. Luplow jumped over the wall and caught Williams's fly ball before landing in the Red Sox bullpen. Seattle's Jay Buhner made a more stationary leap and catch, landing in the bullpen to snatch a homer from Scott Hatteberg in 1997.

Fenway's right field line features a yellow foul pole stationed a hideous 302 feet from home plate. It is affec-

tionately known as Pesky's Pole, named after the lovable Sox shortstop who claims to have curled 8 of his 17 career homers inside it. Carl Yastrzemski ripped a short homer down the line against rocketman Ron Guidry in the 1978 playoff game, but most of the cheapie round-trippers to this corner are hit by banjo right-handed hitters who get behind a fastball and slice it down the line.

The measurement for Pesky's Pole is deceiving because the wall tapers dramatically, and straightaway right field is a more serious 380 feet from home plate. Left-handed hitters have a hard time driving the ball out in right field, particularly in the spring, when the east wind cuts to the bone.

Beyond the right field fence, far up the bleachers, a single red seat—seat 21 in row 37 of section 42—sits in a sea of green. Known simply as "the red seat," it marks the spot where Ted Williams hit the longest measured home run in Fenway's eighty-seven-year history. Like a fleck of red paint on an otherwise lush green canvas, the commemorative chair draws the eye. Someone is almost always sitting there, even when just a few patrons are in the bleachers. When new fans ask about it, the citizens of Red Sox Nation are happy to relay the Fenway folklore. Teddy Ballgame's mighty clout was struck on a windy, sun-splashed Sunday afternoon in 1946 in the first inning of the second game of a doubleheader against the Tigers.

"Hell, I can tell you everything about that one," Williams said when asked about it. "I hit it off Fred Hutchinson, who was a tough rightie who changed speeds real good. Let me tell ya—changing speeds didn't bother me nearly that much. I could pick up the movement of his arm. He threw me a changeup and I saw it coming. I picked it up fast and I just whaled into it."

The ball sailed over the head of Detroit's right fielder Pat Mullin, then carried beyond the visitors' bullpen and kept on going to crash down on top of Joseph A. Boucher's head. More accurately, it landed on Boucher's straw hat, puncturing the middle of the fashionable skimmer. Boucher was a construction engineer from Albany who lived in an apartment on Commonwealth Avenue when he worked in Park Square during the week. Sitting more than thirty rows behind the bullpen, he wasn't expecting to catch any home run

"What's his race or religion got to do with it — HE CAN PITCH!

FIGHT FOR Racial and Religious Understanding

Sponsored as a public service by MASSACHUSETTS COMMITTEE of CATHOLICS, PROTESTANTS and JEWS and BOSTON AMERICAN LEAGUE BASEBALL CO.

Larry Doby, the first black player in the American League, examines a billboard at Fenway promoting racial harmony.

balls on that fateful June afternoon.

Scratching his head, after the game Boucher asked the *Globe*'s Harold Kaese, "How far away must one sit to be safe in this park? I didn't even get the ball. They say it bounced a dozen rows higher, but after it hit my head, I was no longer interested. I couldn't see the ball. Nobody could. The sun was right in our eyes. All we could do was duck. I'm glad I didn't stand up."

The next day's *Globe* featured a page 1 photo of Boucher holding his hat, his finger stuck through the hole. The caption read, "BULLSEYE! . . ."

Newspaper accounts claimed that Williams's homer traveled 450 feet, but the Red Sox measured the distance

in the mid-1980s and arrived at an official count of 502 feet. This doesn't take into account where the ball would have landed had it not been stopped by Boucher's head.

"It's hard to believe anybody could hit a ball that far," said Mo Vaughn, himself a slugger. "I know I've never even come close—not even in batting practice. I mean, it's not even down the line. It's in the gap! You can barely see that thing."

In 1984, the Sox owner Haywood Sullivan decided to commemorate Williams's clout by putting a red plastic seat in the spot where Boucher sat on June 9, 1946. Boucher's grandson, William McGuire of Quincy, said, "You never would find a more devoted Red Sox fan than

Vern Stephens and Walt Dropo with a bevy of beauties, ca. 1950

my grandfather. When he didn't go home to Albany on weekends, he always went to Fenway Park. I used to hop on the train and go meet him when I was a kid. If they ever tear down Fenway, I want first dibs on that seat."

Seven light towers were erected in 1947 when the Red Sox—ever on the cutting edge—became the fourteenth of the sixteen big league teams to play at night. The Red Sox beat the White Sox, 5–3, on June 13, 1947, in Fenway's first night game. In 1953, Yawkey built a runway between the visitors' dugout and the clubhouse. Until then, both teams had entered and exited through a single tunnel, but the system failed when the combustible Billy Martin and even more combustible Jimmy Piersall duked it out after a game in May 1952.

The garage door in foul territory in left field, big enough to accommodate car traffic, has survived several renovations. It stays closed during games, but fair balls hit down the left field line sometimes wind up rattling around the door frame. The players, coaches, and managers in the visitors' dugout (near third base) and fans in the left field grandstand cannot see what is happening when a left fielder disappears into the corner to joust with a baseball bouncing around the door frame. Only at Fenway.

Fenway's center field flagpole was removed from the warning track in 1970, and padding was installed on the outfield walls after the rookie wonderboy Fred Lynn crashed into the center field fence during the 1975 World Series. The electronic mega-scoreboard was

installed in 1976, and forty-four luxury boxes were built, starting in 1982.

Fenway is one of the last major league parks still featuring organ music before and after games and between innings. Most parks have succumbed to ear-splitting rock 'n' roll, bombarding the senses with endless replays of "Louie Louie" and "Twist and Shout." Fenway introduced rock 'n' roll in the 1990s, but the Rolling Stones and the Beatles share time with a Yamaha Electone organ, played by Richard Giglio and Ray Totaro. The late John Kiley manned the Fenway organ for three decades, and veteran fans still get chills when they remember Kiley's bursting into the Hallelujah Chorus after Carlton Fisk's home run off the foul pole in Game 6 of the 1975 World Series. Today it's Totaro (who studied under Kiley and called him "Uncle John") playing "Everything's Coming Up Roses," "On Wisconsin," and "If I Fell" in an effort to please fans of every generation. There's a special play list for rain delays, and Sox homers are applauded by a fanfare ditty that stops when the batter gets to third base.

The last true bleacher seats—wooden planks with no backs—were replaced with plastic seats in 1983, the same year that Fenway's first elevator was built. In 1989, the old press box was gutted to make room for the infamous 600 Club behind home plate, and a new press box was built on top of the 600 Club, giving sportswriters a perch 100 feet above the batter's box—a vantage point normally associated with the Goodyear blimp.

The 600 Club is a monument to change-for-the-worse, a plastic place that takes only plastic. It's a deep-seated chrome and glass theater of cushy seats with cup-holders backed by a monstrous bar and food emporium. There is no fresh air, and the only game sound is piped in electronically. It is as if the ticket-holders are watching the game from inside a fishbowl. The 600 Club is where the seats are always half empty (sold, but not occupied) and hardly anyone watches the game. Wade Boggs and Mike Greenwell, strong Red Sox batters who were unable to otherwise explain their diminishing power in the early 1990s, used the 600 Club as an excuse. They said their home run droughts were caused by an artificial blockage of prevailing winds.

The left field wall and the outfield dimensions are always cited when Fenway is portrayed as a hitter's ballpark, but the lack of foul territory may contribute as much as the cozy fences. A pop-up that would be an out in Oakland is out of play in Fenway. The Fenway hitter lives for another pitch. Over the course of 81 games, this inflates batting averages and RBI totals. It's a double benefit for fans: their proximity to the players contributes to the high-scoring games by eliminating extra outs.

In 1958, Ted Williams was reminded once again just how close the fans are. After striking out against the Washington Senator righty Bill Fischer (later a pitching coach with the 1986 World Series Red Sox), Williams took a vicious cut at an imaginary ball and the bat slipped from his hands. It sailed into the air and crashed down on the head of sixty-nine-year-old Gladys Heffernan, who was sitting in the front row near the Sox dugout. Fortunately, Heffernan was the housekeeper of Joe Cronin, the general manager of the Red Sox, and did not sue Williams or the team.

Fenway has spawned imitators, none more authentic than Bucky Dent's "Little Fenway," off Linton Boulevard next to U.S. 1 in Delray Beach, Florida. Built almost to scale (without 33,000 seats) in 1988–89, Dent's mini-Fenway is the centerpiece of his baseball school, but it also serves as a cruel joke on Red Sox Nation. The numbers on the Little Fenway left field scoreboard represent one of the worst days in Red Sox history, October 2, 1978. It shows

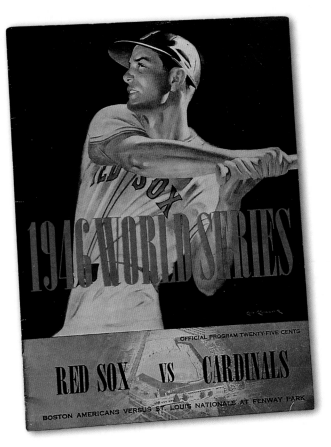

the Yankees leading the Red Sox, 3–2, with New York batting in the top of the seventh inning—the moment just after Dent's three-run pop-fly homer off Mike Torrez ruined Boston's best team of the last half century. On February 13, 1989, Dent imported Torrez for the grand opening of the Fenway replica. Torrez gleefully cooperated, going so far as to throw Dent another gopher ball to christen the park. Dent hit another homer off Torrez. "I'd like to thank Mike Torrez one more time," he told the appreciative crowd. "Without him, none of this would have been possible."

Ouch. It was like watching the captain of the *Exxon Valdez* ramming his oil tanker into shore a second time.

Meanwhile, closer to home, the former Red Sox third baseman Tim Naehring wants to build a $1.5-million replica of Fenway Park on twelve acres next to a landfill in Quincy, Massachusetts. Run by Naehring's Athletes Reaching Out Foundation, it would provide a free ball field for Little League and high school teams.

If you're looking for a scaled-down model, there's a company in Connecticut that will send you an official replica of Fenway Park for $47.50, payable in two monthly installments.

Small wonder that it has spawned imitators. Fenway Park is a friendly neighborhood joint, the corner bar of American sports palaces. The buildings around Fenway are old, the streets cracked, and the stores cater to students and baseball fans. On game day, it feels like a European marketplace outside the park, and the smells whet the appetite for what lies inside. Vendors sell all variety of sausage, chicken, and beef sandwiches. Carnival barkers promote their wares—"Peanuts! Programs! Souvenirs! Sunglasses! Baseball cards! Hot sausages!"—and every fan is assured that the price outside beats the one within Fenway's walls. It's the same with the saloons that rim the park on Yawkey Way, Brookline Ave., and Lansdowne Street. The beer at the Cask & Flagon is sure to be cheaper and richer than the watered-down four-dollar cup sold inside the yard.

And where else but at Fenway can you find a bona fide 1950s bowling alley inside the ballpark? It's true. At the corner of Brookline Ave. and Lansdowne Street, a twenty-lane bowling alley run by Ryan Family Amusements is under the ballpark and features a video arcade and ten pool tables in addition to the candlepin lanes; one package plan includes a tour of the ballpark. On game days, there's a spectacular view of the Fenway traffic on Yawkey Way from the arcade room. The new major league ballpark in Arizona may have a swimming pool (capacity 35), which can be rented for $4,300 per game, but only Fenway allows you to roll a few spares and strikes after watching Pedro Martinez throw strikes upstairs.

IT'S BEEN POPULAR TO TALK ABOUT BASEBALL AS A country game, a sport played by boys in hamlets across America. In New England's factory and mill towns, the game certainly flourished when the teams in neighboring towns would compete, giving folks some cheap summer entertainment. In the 1930s, New England town baseball was as popular as concerts at the town bandstand. Coupled with the fable that the game was invented in little Cooperstown, New York, baseball looks like a Norman

Rockwell magazine cover. There is much legitimacy to the image when one talks about the amateur and even minor league levels of professional baseball. But the big league game was made for and played in big cities. And that is why Fenway Park will always be better than The (new) Ballpark in Arlington, Texas, and the renovated Edison Field in Anaheim, California. Today's new parks in Baltimore and Cleveland (and soon Detroit) are special because they still have the city skyline as a backdrop. They can be reached by subways and buses. They are only a short walk from the downtown hotels. They are part of city neighborhoods, like the old ballparks in Chicago, Pittsburgh, New York, and Philadelphia.

Fenway, surrounded by Boston's medical community and educational institutions, is a city park like none other. From the top of a Fenway light tower, one can see Children's Hospital and the Dana-Farber Cancer Institute, MIT and Harvard, the Massachusetts State House and the Charles River, the Museum of Fine Arts and Symphony Hall, and the old Braves Field, now part of Boston University. One can see the Bunker Hill Monument and Bunker Hill Community College, where Sacco and Vanzetti were executed in 1927, when it was the Charlestown State Prison. One can see the former Hotel Shelton, where Eugene O'Neill died, and Massachusetts Avenue, where Martin Luther King, Jr., lived when he studied at Boston University Divinity School. One can see Simmons, Emmanuel, and Wheelock colleges.

The best part about Fenway is that all of these places can be reached by foot. The worst part is that Fenway is almost impossible to find by car unless you are a veteran Hub driver. Many a Boston rookie—or a player acquired in a trade—has driven 'round and 'round the streets of Boston in a futile search for Fenway. Out-of-towners and once-a-year fans experience the same frustration. It's especially galling when one can see the ballpark but still can't move any closer to the promised land. Traveling east on the Mass. Turnpike, a driver sees the Green Monster to his right and can actually tell who's batting by looking at the giant scoreboard in center, but there is no specific exit for Fenway. One disappears into a tunnel and sees that the next exit is Copley Square. A first-time ticket holder from the suburbs instantly knows the feeling experienced by

Ted Williams, Eddie Pellagrini, and Tiger slugger Hank Greenberg talk baseball with young congressional candidate John F. Kennedy in 1946.

the legendary Charlie on the MTA. You can ride forever on the streets of Boston and never stumble over the famous Red Sox playground.

If you can get your car near Fenway, you still have to face your biggest hurdle: parking. Perhaps the field should be renamed Fenway No-Park because there is no place to beach your car. The Red Sox ballplayers use a tiny lot on Van Ness Street, right outside the Sox clubhouse, but the little lot can't accommodate the twenty-five Jeeps and Land Rovers driven by Nomar and the gang, so the City of Boston allows the team to absorb Van Ness Street on game days. It's an old-fashioned "wink-wink" deal between the ball club and the Boston Police. Signs inform would-be parkers that meters around Fenway are not good two hours before and after a game. Cars that violate the order are either ticketed or towed. A small garage is attached to the park down the right field line, but most fans opt for space at nearby gas stations and fast food outlets, which become Sox parking lots on game days.

There is much about Fenway that is difficult to embrace, yet baseball fans flock to Yawkey Way year after year. To satisfy tourists who visit Boston in the off-season or when the Sox are out of town, the ball club provides official tours of Fenway. When the Sox are down in the standings, they stay up in attendance because Boston has a star ballpark.

Even the players, never a sentimental lot, remember Fenway fondly. Take Bill Buckner, for example. If ever there was a major leaguer who had reason to despise Fenway, it would be Buckner. He's a former All-Star, a batting champion, and collected 2,715 big league hits—but he is remembered only as the man who let a ground ball slither through his legs in Game 6 of the 1986 World Series. Buckner tried to raise a family in Greater Boston after he retired, but too often he was ridiculed for muffing the Little League grounder. He eventually settled in Meridian, Idaho, where he bought a car dealership and worked in real estate. His first real estate project was a subdivision of starter homes, which he named—what else?—Fenway Park.

ROOF
BOX
7-13

I think walking up to Fenway is thrilling.

The approach to it. The smells. You go to Fenway and you revert to your childhood.

You go to Fenway and you think,

"Something wonderful's going to happen today."

— DAVID HALBERSTAM

How far away must one sit to be safe in this park?

I didn't even get the ball.

— Red Sox fan **JOSEPH A. BOUCHER,** who was conked in the head
by Ted Williams's 502-foot home run into the right field bleachers.
A red seat marks the spot where Boucher sat and Ted struck.

As a place of public assembly,

a stadium or ballpark is an expression of the involvement of a community

in the life and passion of the time.

— **WEBB NICHOLS,** ARCHITECT

The big thing about Fenway is the crowd.

When you come out of that bullpen, it's kind of weird.

It's like in the days of the Romans in the Colosseum.

— **DENNIS ECKERSLEY**

Recipe for Fenway grass:

85 percent Kentucky bluegrass, 15 percent perennial ryegrass,

lots of water, lots of love, and keep the fans off the field.

— JOE MOONEY, GROUNDSKEEPER

I take some weird comfort in the knowledge that these poles

are the same poles that blocked the vision of my dad and his dad

when they would take the trolley in from Cambridge

to watch the Red Sox in the 1920s.

— DAN SHAUGHNESSY

Fenway Park is a friendly neighborhood joint,

the corner bar of American sports palaces.

— DAN SHAUGHNESSY

It's like being in an English theatre.

You're right on top of the stage. So chummy.

— TIP O'NEILL

31 ATL   10 HOU
34 CHI   27 SD

Perhaps the field should be renamed Fenway No-Park

because there is no place to beach your car.

— DAN SHAUGHNESSY

Top: Scoreboard operator Chris Elias watches the action from inside the left field wall.

Above: Ancient graffiti inside the Wall commemorates Ted Williams's homers in 1951.

It is a New England landmark, no less so than the Bunker Hill Monument, the

Old Man of the Mountain, or Walden Pond. And when major league baseball is

no longer played in Fenway Park, there is a good chance that the left field wall will

be preserved, either as part of the next park or as a monument to the first century

of American League baseball in Boston.

It was built to keep baseballs in play, but its beauty is the memory of all the balls that have sailed over it. No one knows when the left field wall was first called the Green Monster, but it stands upright as the signature feature of this singular baseball park.

It is probably the Wall's appeal to young people that explains its lasting fame. A six-year-old at his or her first big league game might walk into Camden Yards in Baltimore, Jacobs Field in Cleveland, or even Yankee Stadium in the Bronx, and never remember anything specific about the park itself. But a little kid going to his or her first game in Boston is sure to remember the first breathtaking glance at the huge wall in left field. It's big and green and unlike any facade in professional sports. Children remember the Green Monster the way they remember their first look at the Grand Canyon or the Golden Gate Bridge. Size matters. The Green Monster is impossible to ignore or forget.

More than any quirky feature, the Wall has come to symbolize and encapsulate the Fenway experience. The Boston Garden had its parquet floor (which has been moved to the FleetCenter), Wrigley Field has ivy-covered bricks in the outfield, and Notre Dame football is played in the shadow of the Golden Dome under the watchful

eye of Touchdown Jesus, but Fenway's Wall is the most identifiable feature of any sports venue in America.

When network television cameras broadcast a Red Sox game across the country, fans in Des Moines see the Wall and instantly know that the game is being played in Boston. It's like hearing the chowder-thick accent of Ted Kennedy on a newscast. It's everything Boston.

The Wall is a larger part of Boston's baseball history than Ted Williams or Carl Yastrzemski. It is worshiped by hitters, feared by pitchers, and alternately mastered and butchered by outfielders who want to play its unconventional caroms. Managers have lost their hair trying to make the Wall work in their favor, and too many pitchers and hitters have changed their natural practices in an attempt to take advantage of what the Wall offers and denies. The Baltimore Oriole pitchers used to do an imitation of the short Sox righty Marty Pattin pitching in Fenway. The routine involved staring in for the sign from the catcher, getting the sign, then turning around to look at the Wall and shaking off the sign. Once. Twice. Three times. That was Marty Pattin, scared to pitch with the Green Monster lurking over his right shoulder.

Fenway's left field wall is 37 feet high and capped by a 23-foot screen that prevents balls from peppering the pedestrians and vendors on Lansdowne Street. The Wall

A Montreal player patrols the outfield during a rain shower before the game. The Morse code on the vertical scoreboard stripes spells out the initials

is 240 feet long and was originally constructed from thirty thousand pounds of Toncan iron in 1934. Its reinforced steel and concrete foundation sinks 22 feet below the field.

Signs advertising whiskey, razor blades, and soap covered the Wall for more than ten seasons before it was painted green in 1947. Today Monster Green is a custom blend made by John Smith, a commercial painter in Wilmington, Massachusetts, who inherited the job from his father, the late Ken Smith. The initials of Thomas A.

Yawkey and his wife, Jean, are set in Morse code on its scoreboard. The Wall was rebuilt in 1976: old tin panels were replaced by a Formica-type covering that yielded more consistent caroms and less noise (the tin panels were cut into small squares and sold, the proceeds going to the Jimmy Fund). When the old wall was in place, batting practice shots in an empty Fenway produced a clang; now it's something closer to a thud.

At the foul pole, the Wall is only 309 feet and 3 inches from home plate, but for most of the century the Red

LEAGUE

P		IN	R		P
51	NYM		10		55
19	TOR		15		33
29	ATL				34
	TAM				14
61	FLA				43
	BAI				

...omas and Jean Yawkey, former owners of the Red Sox.

Sox posted a sign that read "315." Club officials refused to allow anyone to measure the real distance, but when the *Boston Globe* snuck into Fenway and came up with the new figure, the Sox grudgingly changed the sign. Major league rules today stipulate that no fence in any new park be closer than 325 feet from home plate, but this will probably be waived if the Sox choose to duplicate the Wall in their next park. The term "grandfather clause" was invented for Fenway Park.

The Wall's massive dimensions make it appear closer than it is, and that, too, is part of its appeal. Baseball fans are dreamers, and most of them played a little hardball in their day. Is there a healthy male in his twenties, thirties, or forties who doesn't believe he could stand in Fenway's batter's box and line a couple of shots off or over the Green Monster?

One of baseball's last hand-operated scoreboards is inside the Wall. There a few part-time Sox employees slide 2-pound 12-by-16-inch numbers into slots to tell fans how the Sox are doing and how things are shaping up around the American League. When there's a pennant race and fans are rooting for the Sox to overtake the Yankees, there can be quite a bit of suspense when the kids behind the green door take down a zero and show them that the Orioles have just scored six against New York in Yankee Stadium. No electronic message board can duplicate this thrill.

The Wall has no permanent bathroom, although portables have been used. It's dark, dirty, and designed for Quasimodo. Rat poison lines the floor. It's boiling in the summertime and freezing in the spring and fall. But the kids get to talk with opposing left fielders, and Ted Williams says some of his favorite Fenway memories are chats with the faceless, Oz-like men behind the scoreboard. Tours of Fenway were instituted in the 1990s, and fans are allowed to duck into the room in the Wall. Some of the graffiti are pretty rough, but if you look hard enough you may find some signatures from members of the ground crew and American League players of the last half century. Walk into this secret sanctuary and the first thing you see is the names of Wall workers Dave Savoy, Jim Reid, and Billy Fitzgerald under the heading "1961 All-Star Game." One can only presume that these three young men manned the big board for the midsummer classic during the John F. Kennedy administration.

"I worked inside the Wall for a couple of summers," recalls Joe Cochran, the equipment manager of the Red Sox. "Not every night, but enough games to know what it's like. One night it was so hot, I wound up working in just my boots and boxer shorts. There's drainpipes out there, and I used to see rats' noses poking through. We had a portable toilet, so that helped. Later, when I'd be in the dugout with the team, I'd call to the scoreboard and

The view from inside the Wall.
Chris Elias says, "It's the best
seat in the house. Any other
ballpark, I'd be standing where
the left fielder is."

tell them the Yankees or Tigers just got ten runs in the first inning. The poor kid would post the ten and the whole crowd would groan." In 1975, the late NBC director Harry Coyle put a camera inside the left field wall. Legend has it that a rat appeared, which froze the camera operator and resulted in the best baseball video clip of all time. The unattended camera was focused on home plate and caught Carlton Fisk waving his arms, willing his fly ball into fair territory. His drive caromed off the left field foul pole, and NBC was rewarded with a clip capturing what *TV Guide* in 1998 ranked as the greatest moment in the history of sports television.

There are plenty of other signatures inside the wall. John Stone and John Giuliotti of the ground crew signed while working the 1986 World Series. To the right of their signatures is the autograph of Jimmy Piersall, a master defensive outfielder and baserunner for the Sox in the 1950s. He became famous when his biography, *Fear Strikes Out,* was made into a major motion picture, starring Anthony Perkins, of *Psycho* fame. Piersall went from Fenway to a mental institution, but in 1957 he was idolized by the kids inside the Wall and they kept track of his home runs, both at Fenway and on the road; the evidence is still there. Other graffiti indicate that somebody inside the Wall logged the home runs hit by Ted Williams in 1951 (there were 30). Meanwhile, there are signatures from current big leaguers: Andy Pettitte, Troy O'Leary, Curt Schilling, Scott Kamieniecki, Darren Holmes, Chuck Crim, Chris Bosio, Chuck Knoblauch, Steve Bedrosian, Scott Erickson, and Tim Salmon. There's a message from Oil Can Boyd—"The Can"—and a marking from Boo Ferriss, 1945–50. There's even graffiti from the turbulent '60s—"Free Angela" and "Stop the War."

According to Joe Mooney, the Sox groundskeeper, the Wall is a fine conductor of heat. When Fenway was buried in snow on April Fool's Day, 1997 (while the Sox were opening the season on the West Coast), Mooney piled snow up against the Wall, claiming it melted faster that way.

In July 1998, the second year of interleague play, the Phillies veteran infielder Rex Hudler made Fenway part of his nostalgic tour. He snatched some ivy from the bricks at Wrigley Field, then went inside the Wall at Fenway and came away with a broken red light about the size of a small satellite dish. Hudler said someday he'll tell his kids that Mo Vaughn hit a screaming line drive right through the light. Hudler also used an old bolt to scratch his name inside the Wall. (The thirty-eight-year-old Hudler was released by the Phillies a day after his Fenway heist.) One can only hope that Barry Bonds and Moises Alou sign their names when the NL Stars come back to Fenway in the summer of 1999.

For decades, the Wall has artificially inflated the numbers of Boston's right-handed batters and encouraged the Red Sox to field a team of slow, big-swinging, righty sluggers. Assembling this kind of team has been done at the expense of speed and fundamentals. The Wall teaches a manager to eschew the bunt, forget the hit-and-run, and wait for the game-breaking, 3-run homer. It has scared generations of left-handed pitchers, and rare is the southpaw who will pitch inside at Fenway (the last Red Sox lefty to win 20 games was Mel Parnell, in 1953). The Wall has encouraged the Red Sox to design teams that have trouble winning away games; historically, the Sox have been embarrassed on the artificial turf of Kansas City and also in Yankee Stadium, where left field is several acres larger than in Boston. The 1949 Red Sox went 61–16 at home but only 35–42 on the road, losing the American League pennant in New York when they dropped the final two games of the season.

Many Sox fans believe that the Wall was the undoing of George Scott in 1968. Scott hit .303 during the Impossible Dream season of 1967 but a year later dropped to .171, with 3 homers. Ask Sal Bando what it did to him during the 1975 ALCS. In the second game of the playoffs, at Fenway, Bando hit four shots off the Wall; at least a couple of them would have been homers in most other ballparks. Bando's harvest was 2 singles and 2 doubles.

American League outfielders have been confounded by the Wall for more than sixty years. There can be little doubt that Carl Yastrzemski was the master of Wall-ball defense. An infielder as a collegian at Notre Dame, Yastrzemski had the coordination, the instincts, and the work ethic to make the Wall work for him. He was among the American League's outfield assist leaders annually until baserunners learned to stop going for two when they clanged one off the Wall. Yaz could decoy better than any outfielder and routinely pretended he was ready to catch a ball that he knew was going to carom off the Wall. Sometimes this would make runners slow down or stop altogether. Yaz had another Wall habit that annoyed some Boston pitchers. When a slugger unloaded on a meatball from a Sox hurler, Yaz would sometimes stand motionless, hands on hips, staring forward as the ball sailed over his head, over the screen, and out toward the Mass. Turnpike. He didn't want to give the hitter the satisfaction of turning around, and sometimes it was a message to a Boston pitcher who may have thrown the wrong pitch to the wrong guy.

"I knew when the ball was going out," said Yastrzemski. "It was something I worked into the decoy. But it used to tick the pitchers off. Bill Monbouquette used to say, 'Can't you at least make it look like you can catch it?' Meanwhile, the ball would be on its way over the fence to a spot three-quarters of the way out to the railroad tracks."

Jim Rice followed Yaz to the left field pasture in 1975 and suffered from comparisons with the Hall of Famer. Rice never got better than average defensively, but he did learn the Wall and its caroms, which give visiting outfielders fits. Earl Weaver, the former Oriole manager, still laughs at the thought of Don Baylor trying to play the Wall when the O's came to Boston. Baylor once got tangled up in the left field corner, trying to corral a ball that was rattling around the doorway in the corner and men in the Oriole dugout (which has no view of the corner) wondered what had happened as they watched the Red Sox runners going around the bases. It was one of those "only in Fenway" moments.

The Wall has a ladder that enables the ground crew to pluck home run balls from the screen above. It's the only fair-territory ladder in the majors. One night in the '50s, Ted Williams and Jimmy Piersall converged under a fly ball in left center. To their surprise, the ball hit the ladder and ricocheted toward center, allowing Jim Lemon to circle the bases for an inside-the-park homer. Another one of those moments came in 1963 when the Sox stonefinger slugger Dick Stuart—a man with all the speed of an ox—hit an inside-the-park home run in

A parking lot attendant across the street from the Wall displays his batting practice harvest.

Fenway. His towering fly to left center hit the ladder, then bounced off the head of the Cleveland center fielder, Vic Davalillo, and rolled to the left field corner. By the time Davalillo ran down the ball in the triangle in center, Stuart had chugged around the bases.

The Wall has made heroes out of hitters like Walt Dropo, Stuart, Tony Conigliaro, Rico Petrocelli, George Scott, Ken Harrelson, Rice, Butch Hobson, Tony Perez, Tony Armas, and Dwight Evans. It has helped the Red Sox draw fans and boast of home run champions. It has created excitement and memories, but it has hurt the Red Sox by artificially inflating the abilities of the ball club. It has tipped the scales of baseball's balance, distorting the product and creating advantages and disadvantages that are patently unfair. Never was this more obvious than on the afternoon of October 2, 1978, when Bucky Dent hit a weak pop-up that plopped into the screen and forever changed the course of Red Sox history.

Dent's home run beat the Red Sox in the infamous one-game playoff of 1978, denying the best Boston team of the last half century its chance to compete in the postseason. It's a cruel joke that a sawed-off shortstop representing the New York Yankees would be the one to use the Wall like no other player in baseball history.

379

The Major League All-Star Game will be played at Fenway Park on July 13, 1999, marking the third time in history and the first time since 1961 that baseball's showcase exhibition visited Fenway. The game will no doubt serve as an opening farewell for those who've accepted the mortality of Fenway and the need for a new ballpark in Boston.

The major leagues' midsummer classic is without question the premier All-Star gathering among the big four professional sports. The NBA and NHL offer mid-winter festivals celebrating the achievements of their stars, but no one ever remembers anything that happened in the games. The NFL's Pro Bowl is a Hawaii boondoggle that receives sparse coverage and deserves less.

But baseball has an All-Star Game that's really a game. Fans vote. They care about who starts and who is named as a reserve. And the fans remember. There is folklore about the baseball All-Star Game. It's where Carl Hubbell struck out five Hall of Fame sluggers in succession (Babe Ruth, Lou Gehrig, Jimmie Foxx, Al Simmons, and Joe Cronin) at the Polo Grounds in 1934. It's where Stu Miller was literally blown off the mound by gusty winds at Candlestick Park in 1961, and where Dick Radatz gave up the game-winning homer to Johnny Callison in Shea Stadium in 1964. It's where Pete Rose steamrolled Ray Fosse at home plate in 1970, where Reggie Jackson hit one of the longest home runs of all time off Dock Ellis in Detroit in 1971. It's where John Kruk batted left against Randy Johnson in Baltimore in 1993.

Babe Ruth hit the first home run in All-Star history. And now it's fitting that the final All-Star Game of this century be played in the park where Ruth got his start.

The 1999 All-Star Game was originally scheduled to be played in Milwaukee's new Miller Park, with Boston promised the game for either 2001 (the hundredth birth-day of the Red Sox franchise) or 2003 (the hundredth anniversary of the Red Sox's winning the first World Series). When it became clear that Miller Park wouldn't be ready, Bud Selig, the owner of the Brewers and now the commissioner of baseball, went to his friend John Harrington, the CEO of the Sox, and arranged a swap. Unless the Red Sox make it back to the World Series before moving to a new park, the '99 All-Star Game will serve as the final national showcase for Fenway.

THIS WON'T BE THE FIRST TIME FENWAY'S BEEN THE site of something more than a Red Sox game. For a time, the park served a number of sports. Like Tiger Stadium, Yankee Stadium, Baltimore's Memorial Stadium, and Cleveland Stadium, Fenway accommodated pro football as well. The Boston Redskins (now in Washington, D.C.) played four home seasons at Fenway in the 1930s, and the Boston Yankees (now the Indianapolis Colts) leased Fenway from 1944 to 1948. From 1963 to 1968, the Boston Patriots played their home games at Fenway. Jack Kemp, the director of HUD, played quarterback at

The All-Star Game comes to Fenway in 1946. The American League team is at top,
the National League team below.

The All-Star teams line up on the baselines at Fenway before the midsummer Classic of 1961.
The game, ending in a 1–1 tie, was called after nine innings on account of rain.

Fenway Park, and middle-age New Englanders still remember the fans pelting Cookie Gilchrist with snow-balls when the Pats played the Buffalo Bills. The Fenway gridiron was horrible for fans: the football configuration ran from the third base line out toward right field, which meant that the left field wall stood where you'd normally place the primo sideline seats. At different times, Boston College, Boston University, Notre Dame, and Dartmouth played college football at Fenway.

Franklin Delano Roosevelt delivered his final campaign speech at Fenway Park in November of 1944, and the park has also been used for basketball exhibitions, soccer games, revival meetings, memorial services, and a jazz festival. The college baseball Beanpot (the better-known hockey Beanpot pits Harvard, Boston University, Boston College, and Northeastern in a tournament each February) is played at Fenway, as are high school baseball playoffs. One day each summer, the Jimmy Fund takes over the park for a massive fund-raiser: for a hefty fee, fans are allowed to stand in the batter's box and take a few whacks at the Green Monster.

The first All-Star Game in Boston was played at

Braves Field in 1936 and produced a 4–3 National League victory, with Dizzy Dean beating Lefty Grove. It was Joe DiMaggio's All-Star debut; Mr. Coffee went 0 for 5 and committed an error.

Fenway's two All-Star games produced a 12–0 American League blowout in 1946 and a boring, rain-soaked 1–1 tie in '61.

The first All-Star Game in Yawkey's yard was played on July 9, 1946, when Ted Williams, going 4 for 4 with 2 homers and 5 RBIs, led the American League to the most lopsided win in All-Star history. The Red Sox were en

route to their first American League pennant since 1918, and eight Boston players—Williams, Dom DiMaggio, Bobby Doerr, Rudy York, Hal Wagner, Dave Ferriss, Mickey Harris, and Johnny Pesky—were on the AL roster. Pesky, Dom DiMaggio, Williams, and Doerr batted 1, 2, 3, 5 in the American League lineup. Joe DiMaggio got hurt in Philadelphia the day before the game and begged off—just like a '90s player.

Even with the large Boston contingent, there was some controversy regarding AL manager Steve O'Neill's selections. The Sox fans wanted to see the Boston righty

Tex Hughson (on his way to a 20-win season), and they also wanted to know why Joe Cronin, the Sox manager, wasn't part of the American League coaching staff. Reporters speculated that Cronin was omitted because he didn't get along with Luke Sewell, the St. Louis Browns skipper, who was part of O'Neill's All-Star staff.

Tom Yawkey threw a huge bash at the Copley Plaza the night before the big game. Ever a friend of the baseball writers, Yawkey treated the press well and had temporary press seating built on the roof of the park to accommodate the two hundred reporters and photographers who invaded Boston for the game. This auxiliary seating eventually became Fenway's permanent roof boxes, still among the best seats at the old yard.

There had been no All-Star Game in 1945 due to the war, so the 1946 game was the first postwar Classic, which meant that the best players in big league ball were back on display. The NL All-Star Frank McCormick, a first baseman for the Phillies, said, "I don't think I've ever seen a more festive occasion than the 1946 All-Star Game. Guys who hadn't seen one another in years were crossing back and forth before the game to shake hands and visit."

Bob Feller—on his way to a 26-win, 348-strikeout season—started for the American League and pitched three shutout innings. Williams's first home run, off the Brooklyn righty Kirby Higbe, went six rows into the center field bleachers in the fourth inning to give the Americans a 3–0 lead. But it was Ted's second blast that made the game memorable.

In the bottom of the eighth inning, with the game hopelessly out of reach for the National League, its manager, Charley Grimm, called for the Pittsburgh righty Rip Sewell. Sewell's best-known pitch was the infamous "eephus" ball. A half century before Jerry Seinfeld turned "nothing" into millions, Sewell confused National League batters with a high, slow parabola that dropped down through the strike zone as if it had fallen from a blimp. Before the game, Williams asked Sewell if he'd dare throw "that damned crazy pitch" in the All-Star Game, and Sewell promised to serve one to the Kid.

So when Ted strode to the plate with the American League leading, 9–0, and two runners aboard, the time seemed ripe for Sewell to have a little fun. On his first delivery, he wound up mightily, then floated an eephus toward home plate; Williams almost hurt himself with a wicked cut that resulted in a feeble pop out of play. Sewell managed to sneak a fastball past Ted for a called strike, missed on another eephus, then tried a third moonball. Williams literally stepped into the pitch and smacked it into the right field bullpen, where it was caught by his teammate, the pitcher Mickey Harris. Ted laughed all the way around the bases. According to Sewell, Williams was the only man who ever hit an eephus for a home run.

The game drew 34,906 to Fenway and was considered a dress rehearsal for the 1946 World Series. The *Globe* ran the box score in big type on page 1, right next to a story about two downtown Boston parking lots that had increased their all-day rate to a whopping one dollar. In other news, Ford Frick, the president of the National League, had his wallet stolen from his hotel room and arrived at the park with only thirty-eight cents in his pocket.

Fifteen years later, the All-Star Game returned to Fenway on July 31, 1961, allowing the Boston fans to watch National League stars for the first time since the Braves left town, after the 1953 season. The Sox representatives included the manager, Mike Higgins, who served as an American League coach, as well as the reliever Mike Fornieles and Don Schwall, who would go on to be named American League Rookie of the Year.

Led by Whitey Ford, player representatives from the eighteen big league teams spent the morning of the game at the Statler Hilton Hotel, drafting a letter that asked the owners to eliminate segregated housing at spring training sites; they cited the west coast of Florida as a trouble spot.

The game itself was nationally televised by NBC, with Curt Gowdy and Joe Garagiola behind the mikes. It did not sell out. Tickets cost six and eight dollars, and only 31,851 saw the American and National Leaguers battle to a 1–1 tie. Commissioner Ford Frick (he had his wallet and a new job by 1961) called the game off after a mere half-hour delay, and there was some grumbling when the skies cleared an hour later. It's the only tie in All-Star history.

Much slugging was expected at Fenway in '61, but

little materialized as seven hurlers—Bob Purkey, Art Mahaffey, Sandy Koufax, Stu Miller, Jim Bunning, Schwall, and Camilo Pascual—held the All-Star batters to a combined total of two runs and nine hits. This was the year in which Roger Maris would hit 61 homers and his teammate Mickey Mantle would add 54. The M&M Boys went 0 for 4 in the All-Star Game. The AL run came on a first-inning homer into the net by Rocky Colavito off a Purkey changeup.

The 1961 National League All-Star lineup had Hank Aaron, Eddie Mathews, Willie Mays, and Ernie Banks, all members of the 500-homer club, but only Mays managed a hit—a single. This game was the only Fenway appearance for Koufax, Mays, Banks, and Roberto Clemente.

The racial composition of the two lineups says much about what was happening in the two leagues. The NL starting nine included three American blacks plus Clemente and Orlando Cepeda, both Puerto Ricans. The AL starters were entirely white with the exception of the Venezuelan shortstop Luis Aparicio. This, in part, explains why the National League would win 11 straight and 18 out of 19 All-Star games between 1964 and 1982. The National League was way ahead of the American League in desegregation, and no franchise lagged behind more than Boston. If Pumpsie Green and Earl Wilson hadn't been promoted in August 1959, Ted Williams could have spent his entire career without ever having a black teammate.

Warren Spahn didn't pitch in the '61 non-Classic, but he was awarded a standing ovation from the fans who remembered his days as a Boston Brave. Spahn said, "This is the greatest thing that ever happened to me in baseball." He didn't pitch because he'd gone ten innings a day earlier, winning his career victory 298. Stan Musial is the only player who took part in both Fenway All-Star games, and the National League has yet to homer in 18 All-Star innings at Fenway.

A lot of offense will be expected when the All-Stars come back to Fenway in 1999. It's unlikely there'll be another 1–1 tie. When the American and National leagues convened in Denver in 1998, they combined for a record-tying 31 hits and a record-breaking 21 runs in a 13–8 AL victory.

As baseball moves into the new century, its All-Star Game has become a monster event. More than a single game, it's a three-day celebration of the game's past, present, and future. All-Star Monday—featuring a home-run-hitting contest and skills competitions—has become a particular favorite of the fans, and no doubt hundreds of ticketless New England baseball fans will gather on Lansdowne Street to fetch contest homers crushed by the likes of Mark McGwire and Juan Gonzales.

The Greater Boston Convention & Visitors Bureau estimates that the '99 All-Star Game will pour $40 million into the city's economy. Some 100,000 All-Star visitors are expected, and the Sox figure they'll need space for more than a thousand members of the media. There will also be a FanFest—an interactive tour of the sport, which is expected to draw up to 125,000 baseball zealots. The event is expected to fill 14,000 hotel rooms in Greater Boston.

"It's a big economic boost for the city, it's not just an All-Star Game," said Boston's mayor, Tom Menino.

In 1998 the president of the American League, Gene Budig, said, "We respect the history of the Boston Red Sox. This is one of the original American League franchises, and history is a very important part of the game. The people of this community deserve the All-Star Game, and the time is right."

It takes two years to plan the game. Major League Baseball provides a twenty-eight-page list of items that the host city must furnish. The Red Sox formed an All-Star Committee in August 1997, and twenty-five members went to Denver for the 1998 Classic at Coors Field.

"Fenway Park has hosted two previous All-Star games, and we felt this was a great chance to honor the tradition and memories it has provided before the century draws to a close," said John Harrington.

Fenway's limited capacity (Boston has 16,000 fewer seats than Denver) means that few Bostonians other than season ticket holders will be able to enjoy the game in person. Major League Baseball gobbles up thousands of tickets for franchise members and corporate sponsors, so they are hideously scarce. The 1999 All-Star Game at Fenway will be the toughest ticket in the history of the ballpark.

David Halberstam

David Halberstam is a Pulitzer Prize–winning author and historian.

I HAD A SPLIT CHILDHOOD. I went to my first game at Yankee Stadium with my father, and he told me to watch the way the great DiMaggio rounded second base. But I had an uncle in Boston named Harry Levy. He cofounded a store in Boston, a wholesale paint store, and he prospered and bought season tickets to the Red Sox games. I remember hearing this during the war, and the idea that anybody in our family would have season tickets was amazing. In '46 he took me to Fenway, and we sat about five rows behind the first base dugout. That was the Red Sox team with Rudy York, Johnny Pesky, Bobby Doerr, and Birdie Tebbetts. I was twelve. It was amazing. You could really see their faces. Rudy York's face was really red. When I go to Fenway now, I can still see the twelve-year-old boy and I can hear my uncle Harry saying, "They're such fine-looking young men." And later in my life I met them and they were such fine men. I don't think I've ever met a better human being in my life than Bobby Doerr.

At that age, you don't know what it is you like about a ballpark. Now I know that what I saw was intimacy. You could see them. You felt connected. And it wasn't just that these seats were very good. Almost anywhere in Fenway you feel connected. There are no distant seats. There really is a feeling of connection and intimacy.

As I grow older, I think of Fenway, and I think of everybody wearing a jacket, a tie, a boater, and maybe Babe Ruth is going to pitch against Smokey Joe Wood. You really think that it goes back in time. I really like the sense of connection in life. I want my daughter to grow up valuing the things I value. I'd love for her in forty or fifty years to fish from Nantucket. I would be thrilled if she lived in the same house. And I love the idea of Fenway, of a connection to the past. When you go there, you're watching where people watched Babe Ruth pitch, where DiMaggio and Williams had their epic battles. It's where Jimmy Foxx and Ellis Kinder and Mel Parnell had their great seasons. I like it when the past reverberates in our lives. Our daughter goes to a great boarding school, and there's nothing more thrilling to me than the Groton chapel. Franklin Roosevelt, Sixth Form (senior class) of 1900. President of the United States, 1933–45. Dean Acheson—Sixth Form of whatever it is—1911, then secretary of state of the United States. Things like that are thrilling to me.

My father introduced me to baseball, so it gives me a great sense of connection. I love Fenway. Even the things that are wrong with it have a quality of humanity. There's a danger in this society of inhumanity, of building parks that are not for fans but are really for tax writeoffs. For basketball, I liked Chicago Stadium better than the United Center. I don't think the FleetCenter is going to be better than the old Boston Garden. I wouldn't want to go to the United Center and have my knees cramped up, but I think it's part of the bargain at a place like Fenway Park. Fenway is very democratic. I don't think the new parks are as democratic because of the price of the ticket. That changes the new parks and arenas. I know the owners have a dilemma, but blue-collar families now can only go once or twice a year.

I didn't go to Fenway games when I was at Harvard. After my childhood experience, I started going again with pals in the 1980s. I went with my friends at the *Globe*. Then I wrote a piece on the Opening Day in 1989 or 1990. It was the first time I had written on deadline in a while. Billy Cleary of Harvard threw out the first ball.

There are certain new things in the world that aren't an improvement. A nice ballpark is a really wonderful thing. And it's so nice to be able to walk to it or take a trolley. I think walking up to Fenway is thrilling. The approach to it. The smells. You go to Fenway and you revert to your childhood. It has a kind of magical quality rather than a functional quality that one generally associates with childhood and the unknown. You go to Fenway and you think, "Something wonderful's going to happen today." Now we're older and you take things in stride, but when you are a kid and you grow up without a lot of money, there's a magical quality to going to a ballpark like Fenway. We didn't have television then, so you didn't take it for granted.

I believe that these temples are our secular cathedrals,

and they tell us as much about what we care about as anything in our environment.

— KEN BURNS

> For years, you had to have a couple of beers in you before you'd eat a hot dog because the hot dogs came out of this murky water that looked like something from the Okefenokee Swamp.
>
> — STEPHEN KING

Stephen King

Stephen King, the best-selling author, is a Red Sox season ticket holder.

DOESN'T EVERYBODY REMEMBER THEIR FIRST TIME AT Fenway? I was twelve years old. We went down from Maine with my cousin, who had his driver's license. It was a gray day. The Red Sox were playing the Tigers. It was either 1959 or '60. Ted Williams was still playing, and Al Kaline was playing for the Tigers. The game was an official game, but it was called after six innings because of rain. Detroit won, and I think Norm Cash hit a home run. What I remember was coming up the runway and out into the park and just being flattened by the beauty of it, by the green. And the day was gray, but the grass was the greenest green I'd ever seen—and I was a country boy.

We sat on the third base side, under the overhang, up pretty high. I didn't have an affinity for Ted at the time because my uncle hated him. My uncle was the kind of guy who'd get two or three beers in him and start saying, "That goddamned Williams. He don't try worth a darn." He was a real Red Sox fan.

Between the ages of twelve and twenty, I probably saw them once a year, and I used to brag because except for that first game—and I don't think it should really count because it didn't go nine—I never saw them lose. I've often thought that I would like to write a story or even a novel where some columnist finds this old guy who's never seen the Red Sox lose. He's been to a lot of games, and they find out that when they bring this guy into the park, they always win, so they prop him up and get to the World Series, and the guy has a couple of strokes and a heart attack and they're still bringing him in. Of course, the kicker is, he dies before the seventh game.

In college, I went to Fenway more. I had an old Ford station wagon, and my friend, who was a real fan, and I would hop into that and make the six-hour drive from the University of Maine to Fenway. It's a hike, but we didn't mind. I didn't become a regular customer until I got enough money to be able to do it. I became a season ticket holder in 1986. I started to do that because I was going down a lot and I was scrounging for tickets. My first season tickets were on the first base line, and we were there for a while. My clearest memory comes from my youngest son, Owen, who's now twenty-one. In '86 he was nine, and he came down for the third game of the World Series on a school night. Oil Can Boyd pitched and we lost the game. Owen was a huge Red Sox fan and he was up late and it had been a stressful day, and as we left the ballpark he started to cry, and I said, "Now you're a Red Sox fan." We joke about it because we have to joke about it, but it hurts and you learn to live with that. I can remember walking up that ramp and him crying. You can't help it. It's not like you're being cruel to the kid, he's a New Englander. He's in New York now, but he still calls up every night and asks, "What's the score?"

In '78, I watched the Red Sox–Yankees playoff game on TV. I canceled classes that year. It's the only time I ever did that. Through hangovers, sexual obsessions, and everything else, that was the one time I canceled anything.

I love Fenway. I love it in spite of the things about it that I hate. It's dirty, it's crumbly. For years, you had to have a couple of beers in you before you'd eat a hot dog because the hot dogs came out of this murky water that looked like something from the Okefenokee Swamp. And you could never get anything to put on the hot dogs. I'd ask if they had any catsup and the guy would say, "We got mustard on the post." And he's giving you that look, that Boston look. And if you like the mustard, that's good. If you don't, too bad. I've sat behind a pole. There was a big game in '85 when I had to do that, and that's when I decided to get season tickets.

The park doesn't work anymore. My seats now are down beyond third base, and there are fans behind the aisle and they lose everything every time someone passes by. If you want a beer, you have to go out and get it. You can't sit in the stands and get a beer. That means you have to be dedicated to the idea of that beer. You have to get up and actually stir around a little bit. People don't complain, but part of that is that people feel they are part of history when they come to the park.

But I love the people who've been there over the years. You get to know the people who are regulars, and they get to know you. I like the old guys that wipe off your seat. They seem like they were there when the club came in. I love all the little nooks and crannies and places to go—the idea that there's a scoreboard and somebody's behind it, putting up numbers. There's no place like it, and it's ours.

With the team, we've had good days and bad days, and we've had teams where the wheels kind of fell off. But we do have the park. I have memories of Wes Gardner pitching a 1–0 shutout and the full moon rising up over the park and Bob Stanley popping out of the stands and grabbing those beach balls and popping them. You can't trade that stuff. When you're younger you think it's nothing and then later on you realize it's a lot.

When they leave Fenway, I'm going to feel bad about it. I think it would make a great baseball monument to keep the park, but I'm sure the economics of it won't work. But if they have to move on, they have to move on. I think the park is too small for them to be competitive in today's business market for baseball. I'm pretty superstitious. I'm a real superstitious guy. I sometimes think they'd leave all this crap behind them if they moved to a different park. Although it didn't help the White Sox much, did it?

I think it's easier to be a traditionalist when you are young. If they move on, I'll know I had it with my kids. It's like players move on. You try to tell people now that there was this guy, Joe Foy, who was our Troy O'Leary, and they don't know what you're talking about. So I'm sorry they're moving on, but I accept the reality of it, and I've got this ace-in-the-hole in the back of my mind that it will never happen because Boston is so goddamned corrupt that it'll be forty or fifty years before they grease enough palms. And furthermore, even once they get going, they will stretch the job out. When they open the new stadium, I'll go in my wheelchair and you can go in your walker. I love Fenway.

Bob Costas

Bob Costas is a broadcaster for NBC television. He still carries Mickey Mantle's baseball card in his wallet.

I THINK THE FIRST TIME I WENT TO FENWAY WAS THE summer of 1978. I'd seen a zillon games on TV there from growing up in New York. In '78 I was visiting a cousin who I grew up and played ball with. He was a medical student who had his residency at Mass. General, and we went to the Red Sox game together. I knew I would like it. I liked all the old ballparks. I expected it to be great and it was, but even watching a game on color television can't prepare you for the vividness of it—how striking the colors are. We sat on the first base side, kind of two-thirds of the way up, 10 feet beyond first base, down the right field line. It was June or July, and the Red Sox were in control at that time.

There was a big difference when I started going there professionally. When you go there professionally, you want to capture it to some extent and be respectful of it. The most striking thing about it, professionally, which isn't true anymore, is how close the press box and the broadcast booth were to the field. When I did the Game of the Week there with Tony Kubek, Boston and Detroit were the two places where you felt the most in the game. You really felt like you could see the expressions on the players' faces. You just felt in it. Of course, it's not like that anymore since they built the 600 Club and the new press box.

I did the Game of the Week for seven seasons and probably four games a year there, so I probably saw about 25 games. Then I was the host for NBC during the World Series in 1986. We used to stay at a hotel near the park and we could walk over. You get the whole ballpark feel. It reminds me of when I used to go to Yankee Stadium. I would take the subway and get off the elevated subway and go down the trellis, and you'd be right there in the ballpark community. There used to be a place called Manny's Baseball Land that had all the souvenirs, and Baseball Joe's was a great place to get hot dogs. Fenway still feels like that. I don't know the names of the places, but I know you cross over a certain street and you're in baseball territory.

When it comes to ballparks, I think that going new is inevitable. The question is, "How do you go new?" In Baltimore they didn't face quite the same thing as in Boston because as nice as Memorial Stadium was, it was not the monument that Fenway or Wrigley or Yankee Stadium is. In Baltimore, they didn't have to worry about preserving the Green Monster, or the Yankee Stadium facade, or the ivy in Wrigley Field. You would have to do that in any new Yankee Stadium, Wrigley Field, or Fenway Park. But I think ultimately if you get the right deal and it's the right combination of ballpark funds, corporate funds, and public funds, you might as well go the Camden Yards–Jacobs Field route and have the new ballpark reflect the spirit and feeling of the old ballpark. You don't hear it as much about Wrigley Field, but I think part of that is because they have their own television revenue in Chicago, plus the Red Sox are in a division with the Yankees and Orioles and Blue Jays. The Sox may feel like they can't compete without a new park.

I took my son to Fenway the day the strike began in 1994. We saw a doubleheader between the Red Sox and the Indians, and the next day Larry Cancro took us around the stadium. My son, Keith, was eight. We walked about the warning track and I took pictures of him jumping up, pretending to make catches up against the Wall and the bullpen. We went inside the scoreboard, and I told him the story of the rat with Harry Coyle and Carlton Fisk. I've still got the pictures. Keith understood what the deal was. He said, "This is so close. Dad, if this was batting practice, could you hit one over this?" I told him maybe I could hit one to the base of it. The Wall gives everyone that feeling, I think.

I remember standing outside the clubhouse at Fenway. There was this little staircase and they had this sofa sitting at the bottom of the steps, and it had coils and springs coming out of it. And you'd go inside the clubhouse and see Jim Rice and Roger Clemens and you'd think, "This looks like a high school locker room." And Ralph Houk would be sitting in his office, and it looked like the office that the coach had for the Syracuse Blazers when I covered the Eastern Hockey League. Then you'd see the dripping pipes on the way to the dugout in the little tunnel.

But when we lose Fenway, we lose the sense—and

But when we lose Fenway, we lose that sense that

somebody sat here and watched Ted Williams hit.

— BOB COSTAS

Fan Appreciation Day at Fenway.

some people laugh when we say this—but you lose the sense that somebody sat here and watched Ted Williams hit. Somebody sat here and watched Jimmy Foxx and Lefty Grove and Babe Ruth. There's something to be said for that. I always felt it from the day I was a kid, and it's something you just know—like an immutable law of nature—you're ten years old and you're not an intellectual, but you just know when you watch the Mets on TV they were playing in Connie Mack Stadium or Sportsman's Park or Crosley Field. And instinctively, in 1970, you could see that Riverfront Stadium in Cincinnati had more seats than Crosley Field, but in your mind Crosley Field was a much bigger place. I remember thinking that as a teenager. There was no sense of place in those stadiums. Riverfront wasn't any more Cincinnati than it was Pittsburgh or St. Louis. Fenway is just genuine and authentic.

Don Zimmer

Don Zimmer was manager of the Red Sox for five seasons and has been in professional baseball for five decades.

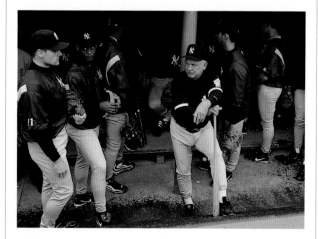

I'VE BEEN IN BASEBALL FOR FIFTY YEARS, AND THE first time I saw Fenway was when I made the All-Star team in 1961. Danny Murtaugh chose me as an extra man. All second basemen that year were having bad years. That was one of the years they had two All-Star games, one in San Francisco and one in Boston. I walked into Fenway for the first time, and being a right-

handed hitter, it looked very inviting.

Fenway has always been a special place for me. People have asked me in the last ten or fifteen years about my favorite parks, and I've always said one was Fenway and the other was Wrigley Field. When I stop and look back, I always say I'm a lucky man. Baseball was something I wanted to do all my life, and I got to manage at both Fenway and Wrigley Field.

There's a difference when you manage in those parks. Fenway and Wrigley are two of the toughest parks to manage in. In Fenway, it's the left field fence. You manage differently. When the wind is blowing out, why give up an out in a bunt situation? You know the score is gonna wind up 10–8 or 13–12. In Boston I ran less because I had a good offensive lineup. There were some left-handed pitchers that had great success there. Bill Lee won 17 games three straight years. Roger Moret. I was never scared of pitching a left-hander in Fenway.

You really get an education coaching third base in Fenway Park. Without a doubt, it's the toughest park in America to coach third in. First of all, you got men on base and they are running, and a guy hits a ball over the third base bag and you're ready to send two or three guys home, and the ball hits that wall that sticks out and bounces out to shortstop . . . or it gets by the Wall and gets all the way down in the corner, and you almost have to go out on the playing field to see where the ball is. I probably went into fair territory a few times to see what was going on.

I coached third there for parts of three seasons. We had a good club and the fans were great fans. They were close. No question about it. In the sixth game of the World Series in 1975, Pete Rose was playing third base, and we had the bases loaded and nobody out and I had told our runner on third, Denny Doyle, that anything that looks like a line drive, get back to the base. The next ball was hit up high to left and I told him to tag up. When I realized it wasn't far enough to take a chance, I ran back to third base and said, "Don't go anywhere." Then I saw him take off and I thought he was faking. I hollered, "No, no, no!" He came up with a story that he thought I said, "Go, go, go!" Ask Pete Rose. He heard me. If we had lost that game, I had planned to leave early so that Denny wouldn't be put on the spot. Fortunately, we won the game. I remember twice during that game Pete told me, "Win or lose, this might be the greatest game I've ever played in."

They all talk about Fenway Park being a hitter's park, but whenever there's an advantage, somewhere along the line there's a disadvantage. A lot of guys hit a line drive that would be a home run anywhere in baseball and it goes for a single in Fenway, off the Wall. Then you hit a high fly ball that's in the net. Here's an advantage for a pitcher. You're winning, 2–1, in the eighth inning. You strike out the first two hitters and the next guy hits a double. Then the next guy singles to left and the third base coach can't send him home. So because you're in Fenway, you get another chance to get out of the inning.

In '78 we had that big lead and we stopped hitting. The Yankees caught us and went ahead of us. People said we choked and were gone, and for a time it looked like we were. Then we won our last 8 games and tied them. When I went to the park Monday morning, at around 7:30 A.M. for that playoff game, it was about the biggest thrill I'd ever had. Just thinking of getting into that park and playing that game. And probably the biggest disappointment I've ever had was losing that game. It looked like we had the game won two or three times. Unfortunately, we didn't win. Lou Piniella caught that ball in the sun in right field (Jerry Remy's one-hop single in the ninth), and to this day he doesn't know how he caught the ball.

The Dent homer I remember like it was yesterday. Usually in October at Fenway the wind would be blowing in. It would be cool. On that day it was warm and the wind was drifting out a little. When you're in that park every day for five years like I was, usually you know where the ball is going when it's hit. When Dent hit that ball, I said, "Good, that's an out." Then I saw Yaz going back, and when he turned around, I said, "Well, that ain't so bad, it's off the Wall." Then the ball went in the net.

That was something. We won 99 games and got to the playoff game. The next year we open at home with Cleveland, and I take out the lineup card and Dave Garcia's there for the Indians. When I walk out of the dugout I got booed by thirty thousand people. Garcia looked at me and said, "I don't think I could take it here.

I really feel bad for you."

You got to do something awful bad to get booed in Chicago. Fenway's different. I learned to live with the fans. I really believe that Bill Lee started most of that. He'd go to the media. He made up names for me. He went to the bullpen and had all those hoodlums out there. I think that rubbed off on some of the fans and they started booing, and it became somewhat of a ritual. I learned to live with it. I can remember one night when my daughter came to the game with my wife. My daughter was a grown woman by then. We were driving home on Route 93 over the bridge and I heard my daughter sniffling. I said, "What the hell is going on?" I looked in the back seat and she was crying like a baby. She said, "Daddy, I'm so tired of you getting booed." I told her to stay home if that was going to bother her.

At Fenway, the fans in the cheap seats would come from way up high, down by the dugout to get me. I never fought with 'em. They'd call me a bum, and every now and then I'd look up at them and say, "You know something, you may be right." I worked in Fenway for seven years. In fifty years of baseball, that's the longest I spent in any place. I had so many friends there. It's still one of my favorite parks, but I think the time has come and they're gonna have to do something. I just think it's gotten old. The seats aren't wide and you got to keep up with the times. It's old. Look what the new parks have done to Baltimore and Cleveland.

George Steinbrenner

George Steinbrenner has owned the New York Yankees
for more than a quarter century.

WHEN I WENT TO WILLIAMS, WE NEVER MADE A DAY trip to Fenway for a game. I came to Boston a lot, but not to Fenway. I always went to the Boston Garden to run track. We came into North Station in our track suits. My first time at Fenway was the first time I had the Yankees, back in 1973. The Boston fans were throwing nuts and bolts at our players in the outfield. Our fans retaliated back in New York. It got very ugly. I like to sit upstairs because I can see the whole game, but I've sat behind home plate with my players' wives, and I've sat in my box several times.

I sat right by the dugout when we came here for the playoff game in 1978. I wanted to be with my players. The day before we had lost to Cleveland's Rick Waits. Luis Tiant won here, and they told us that we had to go to Boston. I was really down. Walking out of the stadium, I saw Ron Guidry standing out in the parking lot with his little baby and wife

and he said, "Relax, I'm going to do it for you." I came up to Boston the next morning by tourist. We couldn't get the first-class section. It was one of the greatest games I've ever seen. Don Zimmer was the Boston manager, and I was waving at him because he was a friend of mine from Florida, but he wouldn't pay any attention to me. Ted Kennedy came to the game and so did Boston's mayor, Kevin White, who was a Williams classmate. Kevin came over and said, "Good luck." Tip O'Neill was there, but he wouldn't do that.

I remember when Lou Piniella made that catch in the sun in the ninth inning and that was the play of the game. It was a great game. No matter who won or who lost. Yaz came up at the end, and I was always uncomfortable when Yaz was hitting, but Goose was on. It was a great match. Yaz skyed it to third base and Nettles caught it. This is probably the best rivalry in sports, certainly one of the top two or three. That's why we are both so wary of

dealing with each other. The summer is always better when the Red Sox are good and the Yankees are good.

They say a left-hander can't win in Fenway, but that is a fallacy. Mel Parnell won here. He was a great pitcher. We came in here one time with Guidry, Dave Righetti, and Tommy John. We came out with three wins because of three left-handed pitchers. Tommy told me that in all his years here, he never had a home run hit over the Green Monster.

Fenway is a little like Yankee Stadium. It's quirky with that wall out there, but in my opinion it's time for a change. Location is an advantage for Boston. This is a decent location. Here, you can walk to the park. But time marches on. Sure, you appreciate certain parts of this old park, but when you get your new stadium, it's the focal point of everybody's life. The tourists and people who come here just to see Fenway will come to a new ball-park. There is nostalgia here, sure, but it's not the same grass, it's not the same players. You think those old players, Ruth and Williams, you think they ran on this grass? No way. Fenway probably has the same urinals, though. That's about the only thing that hasn't changed. They're the same troughs that guys were using in the old days.

You hate to part with Fenway, but if you want to stay competitive with everybody else in baseball, you gotta do it. It's been a great baseball experience here, but every team in the American League has gotten a new stadium except Boston and New York. You need a new stadium to be competitive. New York City is the largest city in the world and it's on a roll. Crime is down, everything is up with the city. We've got a decent team, but we're sixth in attendance. Boston's got a decent team and it's seventh in attendance. It doesn't sound good for either Boston or New York. And all those other cities have money for schools and highways and they still got the new stadium.

George Will

George Will is a syndicated columnist and best-selling author.

I THINK THE APPEAL OF FENWAY PARK IS THAT, LIKE life, it's unfair. Obviously it favors some skills and players and severely punishes others. But the alternative to that is boredom. There's a lesson there about society. Just as we're multiplying laws, year after year, to fine-tune the fairness of life, we find things like Camden Yards that build an element of randomness into it to appeal to us more. It's not just the angles but the radically different distances that you have to hit the ball to get it to the seats. Fenway is a more eccentric ballpark than even the Polo Grounds was. Fenway has more eccentricities built into it. It is, however, a monument to the economics of baseball during the first eight decades of this century, when radio broadcasting and ticket sales were the principal means of supporting the team. This is not the case anymore.

Camden Yards has led the way in this. I really do believe that Camden Yards is the most important thing to happen in baseball since Jackie Robinson, for a lot of reasons. One of them is that baseball has discovered that the ballpark itself is the principal source of revenue. Fenway Park simply can't sustain the various things like restaurants, concessions, and most important, the skyboxes needed to generate the revenues that become starting pitchers and middle infielders.

I remember the night I enjoyed most in Fenway. It was in 1990 and I was here in connection with my book *Men at Work*. The Sox were playing the great A's team of 1990—Steinbach, Lansford, Weiss, Gallego, McGwire, Canseco, Henderson, Henderson, and Stewart. And the A's at that time had that tremendous swagger. It was just terrific—a mini-dynasty in this great setting.

I don't think you overromanticize Fenway Park, but you have to say there's a point at which romance ends. You have to put yourself in a position of someone trying to run the Red Sox, particularly someone trying to run the Red Sox in the American League East, where you have three money machines—Toronto, the Yankees, and the Orioles. And it really requires an act of mature judgment on the part of Red Sox fans. Would they rather lose in a jewel or win in a rhinestone? Besides, the choice for Red Sox fans isn't Fenway Park or Three Rivers Stadium. It's Fenway Park or Fenway Park Updated. I'm not sure why we're not hearing this about Wrigley Field in Chicago, but it seems quite plausible that the economics of the Cubs, being owned by the Tribune Company and being programming for a superstation, makes it less important for them to build sources of revenue in the ballpark.

I have a fairly strong emotional attachment to Tiger Stadium. It may be the best of the old ballparks in terms of shoving you into the intimacy of the game. I taught at Michigan State in 1967–68. I never saw a game at the Polo Grounds or Crosley Field. I saw my first game at Forbes Field in 1950. It was an urban setting, with the so-called Tower of Learning of the University of Pittsburgh hanging over it. In a way, it was an absurdly designed ballpark. I thought Baltimore's Memorial Stadium was a wonderful place to watch a game. There were two things wrong with it: no parking and no skyboxes. I remember flying back from Boston on Ed Williams's private plane. He was in Boston getting treated for cancer. We're flying over Baltimore. He goes to a window, looks down, and says, "No parking," then sits down again.

People always talk about baseball being a pastoral game. Baseball was invented in the Boston and New York areas. It's an urban game; one of the first games was played in what's now the Murray Hill section of New York. It's a little meadow where I guess Cartwright made out a diamond. So baseball's always been an urban game. It helped teach urban workers how to relax and how to play. A nation of go-getters learned how to have recreation by going to ball games. Baseball's appeal to generation after generation of fans is directly related to the fact that it produces, year after year, this tremendous sediment of statistical and other memories. The ballparks simply acquire an aura for having been the scene of where all this stuff is generated—familiar photographs, familiar voices. I mean, here you are in Fenway, where the public address announcer [the late Sherm Feller] was famous. Is there any other place where you can have a PA announcer be a star?

Baseball's a game in which you can really have a meaningful argument as to whether a player in the '20s was a good as one in the '90s. I don't think you can have that argument about football or basketball. They're different games played by different physical specimens. And again, that comes back to why the ballparks matter to us—because exactly comparable people played a comparable game in this ballpark for generation after generation. A Civil War historian once said that if you took someone from McKinley's era, the end of the nineteenth century, put him down in a ballpark today, he'd see differences, but he'd see the same thing. He'd say, "Yeah, I know what's going on." It's the same game.

What two teams are emblematic of long-distance failure? It's the Cubs and the Red Sox. The Red Sox are relative newcomers to this club, having won in 1918. The Cubs last won in 1908, which is two years before Mark Twain died. The similarities are that these two teams play in parks that are made for offense. Offense wins games, defense wins championships. It's an old axiom of many sports. And it does tempt you to build a skewed ball club in a skewed ballpark.

You don't play in a football stadium. You play on an absolutely identical swath of grass, marked off in an absolutely identical way. So the parameters of the venue don't influence the outcome of the competition. The parameters of any ballpark affect the competition, whether it's ivy in Chicago or the Wall in Boston.

Dennis Eckersley

Dennis Eckersley pitched in the major leagues from 1975 to 1998. He will be eligible for the Hall of Fame in 2004.

To me, FENWAY IS WHERE I LEARNED WHAT BASEBALL is all about. What did I know? I'd been in Cleveland. If you're just talking about pitching, Fenway's not good. I've seen a lot of things happen there that wouldn't happen anywhere else. They say left-handers can't pitch there, but that's not true. But if you pitch there long enough, it's going to take its toll. There's no foul territory. I'm a flyball pitcher, and sometimes you can't overcome that. It could come at a key point. You got two outs and there's a pop-up that would have been caught anywhere else, but it's in the stands at Fenway, and then the next pitch is a double. It can be devastating. I think you have to be a power pitcher to pitch there for a long time. You cannot be a finesse pitcher. Put Greg Maddux in this son-of-a-bitch and let's see what he can do. As great as he is, he would not be as good as he is now.

More than anything, I think left-handed hitters can do well there, especially if they can stay behind the ball like Yaz did and Fred Lynn and Mo Vaughn today. Left-handed hitters are tougher than right-handers. They take away the outside part of the plate, so you pitch them in and make them pull the ball. But nobody pulls the ball anymore. I got away with it. The first year I was there [1978], I was 11–1. I don't know why. I said I was letting left-handers pull the ball, but I didn't know. I was lucky.

The big thing about Fenway is the crowd. That's how it begins when you are a starting pitcher. It's especially true the first time you go there as a visiting pitcher and warm up in the bullpen. When you come out of that bullpen it's kind of weird. It's like in the days of the Romans in the Colosseum. When you're going good, they sort of cheer as you're coming out of that gate. If you're not going too well, they hoot on you.

The bullpen crowd was crazier twenty years ago. Years ago, I could smell weed out there. And it's loud, even though it's wide open. It can be intimidating for an opposing player, and it can help the home team. People don't realize that it's not like that in all ballparks. In Oakland the crowds didn't mean anything. Fenway is

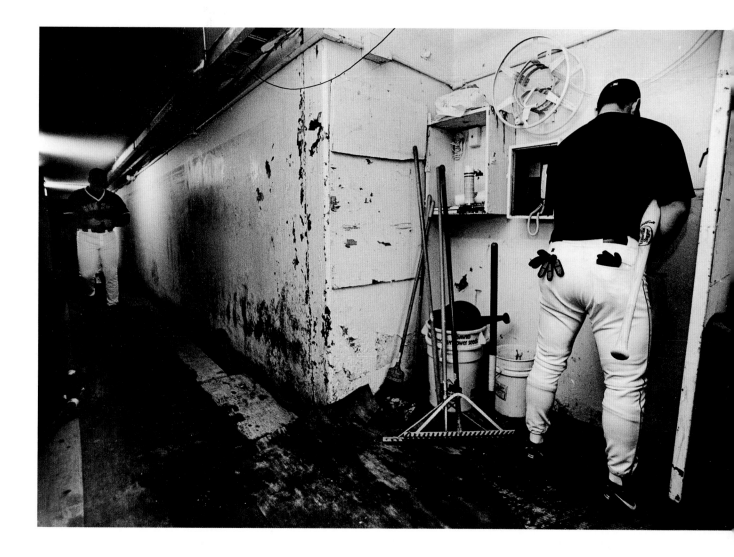

Fenway probably has the same urinals, though.

That's about the only thing that hasn't changed.

They're the same troughs that guys were using in the old days.

— GEORGE STEINBRENNER

Red Sox catcher Scott Hatteberg uses the facilities in the runway
that connects the dugout with the clubhouse.

loud. Maybe it's because they're right on you. The only place you can hide is right field. Everyplace else, they're right on you. There's no other park like that.

Not to hoot on the Boston owners—I know they can't knock out walls or anything—but the player facilities at Fenway are ridiculous. I left for fifteen years and came back and nothing had changed. They added a little weight room. And when you've been to all these state-of-the-art ballparks, it's a joke. More than anything, you just have to change. You have to go with the times. I'd like to see them play there forever, but you can't. The home team doesn't want to play there because compared to every other park, it's not good. If I was a hitter, I wouldn't want it to change. So what if the clubhouse is crap? I could live with that as long as I could hit .330. In the '86 World Series, I had seats down the right field line, turned the wrong way, looking left the whole game. And I was happy.

I like driving to Fenway now. When I first came, I was intimidated by the aggressive people. It was scary. Fenway is the most cramped. Like our player parking lot. You don't bring your nice car, 'cuz it'll get waffled.

I look at Fenway more now than I did when I was young. It's kind of cool. I think you have to get older to appreciate things like Fenway. I played at Wrigley and they've tried to change things, but the Red Sox haven't done anything to Fenway. I went to their organization offices and even those were brutal. Then I went to the 600 Club and felt like I was at the dog track. I hear the next park is going right next door. That'll be a mess. It'll be like the Big Dig. It'll be done when the Dig is done.

Jim Palmer

Jim Palmer was the only pitcher to win a World Series game in three different decades. He was inducted into the Hall of Fame in 1990.

I MET BILLY CRYSTAL IN THE EARLY '90S. *CITY SLICKERS* had come out, and when I saw him I reminded him of the great scene when they were all riding on the horses and they talked about your best day ever. In the movie, Billy talked about his dad taking him to Yankee Stadium and walking him through the tunnel and him seeing how green the grass was. Well, back in the late '70s, we [the Orioles] came to Boston on an off day, a Thursday. We were playing the Red Sox over the weekend. [Coach] Elrod Hendricks told me he'd meet me at Fenway around five o'clock to throw. So there I was, sitting in the outfield of an empty Fenway. There was not one person there. Not one. No guards. No Joe Mooney. I had come out early to do some running and I was sitting in the outfield, stretching. You could smell the ballpark. And there I am on the outfield grass and it's one of those 75-degree days with no humidity and a slight breeze and the sun is shining and the grass is glistening and I'm saying, "This is what it's all about."

The greatest day ever.

When I would come to Boston, I used to run up the ramp to see which way the wind was blowing to see if my neck would hurt from watching the home runs. Fenway is hitter friendly, obviously. It's a challenge to pitch in. It's about tradition. You think about all the great players that ever played there. I sit in Camden Yards, which is a wonderful place to play baseball, but it doesn't have the history. When we left Memorial Stadium, I said I just hoped the new place has as many good things happen as Memorial Stadium did.

Can you imagine taking a sleeping bag to Fenway Park and staying there at night and having the ghosts come and visit you? Just think of all the great players that played left field. And all the great games. That's what this game is all about. For me to have my whole career start there is really something.

My first game in the majors was at Fenway Park. I was nineteen. Robin Roberts was thirty-eight and he was my roommate. We were staying at the old Kenmore Hotel in Boston. I remember going out to dinner the night before and he picked up the check and I couldn't believe it. It was my first time in Boston and I loved it. Dave McNally and I hooked a ride on the MBTA because I'd always heard that song by the Kingston Trio—"Charlie on the MTA." I'd heard about the Wall, too. But I wasn't thinking about too many things. When you are nineteen, you're just happy to be there.

It was Opening Day in Boston and Robin started and we were ahead, 4–3, in the second inning and Hank Bauer called me in to face Tony Conigliaro with the bases loaded. I think it was snowing. I was nervous. When I got to the mound, Bauer asked me if I was nervous, and I said, "No, but what do I do with this extra ball?" I had carried the warm-up ball in from the bullpen. I threw Tony two high fastballs and he swung and missed both. Then I threw him a knee-high fastball and he took it and John Flaherty called it a strike. That was my introduction to Fenway Park. Later in the ball game, I threw a pitch up and away to Felix Mantilla, and he hit a pop fly down the left field line into the screen. The next time he came up, I accidentally threw a ball inside, and he swung so hard and splintered his bat so much they almost had to call the ground crew out to pick up the pieces of his bat. So I learned how to pitch in Fenway in my first game. It's funny, though. I never gave up a grand slam in 3,948

innings and could have given one up to the first batter I ever faced.

The fans in Boston are special. They want the Red Sox to win, but I think more than any town in baseball they respect the athletes that come in. Fans in Boston, because of the great job the newspapers did, and the closeness in the ballpark, it was like you were one of them. I always felt the fans there were really important, like a tenth man. It's the only place I ever pitched where the fans stood up on every fly ball because of the closeness of the fences. If you had a weak heart, you couldn't pitch there. You better get some runs and be on your game to win there. It's a park that tests you emotionally. Good pitchers a lot of times get hit. So it tests you physically and emotionally. You're going to experience some frustration. Our outfielders had trouble there. Don Buford had a ball go through his legs twice in left field. It skipped through once, then he turned around, and it came off the Wall back through his legs again.

The clubhouse was rough. When I first played, the only food they gave you was popcorn and Pepsi. Later, we got the leftover hamburgers from concessions. But it was Fenway Park. It was cramped, but you know what—when you're talking about clubhouse chemistry and being together, there's nothing like the locker room in Fenway Park. I think these clubhouses in the new parks today are too big, too sprawling. You don't even know who's getting dressed around you. You don't see your teammates.

At Fenway, you'd walk through the fans to get to the clubhouse, and when I go back now as a broadcaster it's like you're still playing. The people there just have tremendous respect for baseball, and I think the ballpark has a lot to do with it. Where else can you walk from your hotel downtown and get to where you're going to play?

Ken Burns

Ken Burns is a documentary filmmaker. His nine-part series on baseball filled a void during the 1994 strike.

I GREW UP IN DELAWARE AND MICHIGAN, AND MY FIRST ballpark was Memorial Stadium around 1959. It was a Cub Scout trip. The only local World Series victory I've ever had was with the Tigers in 1968. Growing up in Ann Arbor and being a hippie in the late '60s, baseball— the passion of my childhood—seemed to be no longer relevant. I remember '68 being the last Series I really followed. Baseball seemed out of fashion for me. Then I went to a hippie college in western Massachusetts, Hampshire College, and I remember that the husband of one of my teachers would watch Red Sox games. I had not kept up with anything the Sox had done since '67. But it seemed to be this guilty pleasure that he partook in, and I suddenly got very interested in following the Red Sox, and it was like discovering an old friend that you had forgotten. That was baseball.

I believe passionately that you should root for the team that is local, and since I came to college in 1971, the Boston Red Sox have been my team. I graduated in 1975, and that was a perfect time to come back to baseball. I can still tell you exactly what I was wearing, where I was, and how foolishly I behaved on that incredible night when Fisk hit the home run.

My first time in Fenway was in the late '70s, just going there on a beautiful, hot summer day. I took in a doubleheader against the Twins, and it was all the usual characters—Rice and Lynn and Evans in the outfield. I had Siberian seats on the left field side, but I made an effort to come in, which I always do in a new park, behind home plate. I always remember the green of the grass and the green of the place, and it's still like that. I believe that these temples are our secular cathedrals, and they tell us as much about what we care about as anything in our environment. They break up the grid of the city in a really interesting way. I love the fact that in Fenway Park I'm always sort of geographically disoriented. I've got the Citgo sign and the Pru, but I still am off the normal grid, and I love that.

I think I was always surprised at its intimacy. When you see these places on TV or in photographs, the camera lies and gives it a size that it doesn't really have. There's something great about the small parks that have that instant intimacy, and I've had some of the greatest experiences of my life in that park. I went to Opening Day in 1998 with my daughter. We sat in left field Siberia, behind a post. The Mariners were beating us, 7–2, in the bottom of the ninth, and we won, 9–7. Mo Vaughn won it with the grand slam. I've never been as high as that day. When my daughter was six months old, in the spring of '83, I took her to a Red Sox game, her first, and we sat behind home plate and Tony Armas hit a grand slam, and she started screaming and wailing because everybody else was doing that.

I like the Fenway people most of all. For my film *Baseball,* I interviewed a Fenway usher who works in a computer lab at MIT by day. He's a Cuban refugee who must be in his seventies now. The interview made it into the film. It was beautiful. Since the baseball series came out, I can't walk in there without having ten thousand conversations. The people are part of my congregation, and I like going to church. I love the color. And I love the Red Sox, no matter what they do, or how foolish they behave, or how bad or good they are.

As for the future, I'm in two places about this. I believe in cherishing and preserving the old, and I don't want anything to happen to Fenway Park. Yet when it was built, there was a huge architectural act of faith going on in baseball. Baseball was threatened, just as we perceive it is now. Despite that, it had an incredible architectural rebirth. That's when Ebbetts Field was built, and that's when Fenway and Wrigley and all these great stadiums were built. And it revitalized baseball.

Now, there's been another incredible architectural act of faith going on that began with Camden Yards and continues with the Jake and Arlington and Coors Field. And one wonders what kind of inspiring energy would be brought to the city if the Sox had that? And at the same time, you don't want to tear down the old church. I'm really torn. I love the place, and it's the scene of some of my saddest and happiest memories.

James Earl Jones

James Earl Jones appeared in the 1989 film *Field of Dreams*.

I GREW UP IN MICHIGAN. AT THAT TIME BASEBALL WAS still segregated, so I didn't really go to see baseball. We had traveling teams in our county and I'd go to those games, but not the major leagues. I was never a major league baseball fan.

I came to Fenway Park in association with *Field of Dreams*. It didn't make me a baseball fan, but it made me understand and appreciate the game. I had not been to Fenway before. I had heard about it from [the film critic] Jeffrey Lyons, who is a staunch Red Sox fan. He can't say enough about Fenway.

When you walk into that stadium, you fall in love with the grass. You fall in love with that field of dreams and the design, and I think every stadium in the country should have some of that. It's a wonderful place. I also noticed how close it is to the city and the nature of the fans.

We didn't go on the field. We just stayed in the stands. We were only there one day. We had a small group of extras who sat behind us and in front in our section. Most of the time, Kevin Costner and I were relating to the scoreboard. He'd say, "Did you see that?" and I'd say, "What?" There was no ball game at the time we were shooting. You cannot ask professional players to keep repeating the way actors do.

The movie was definitely about baseball and about fathers and sons. Bart Giamatti's books have the same kind of poetry as Kinsella's. I don't know if they ever knew each other. My wife always read scripts, and she read that script and said, "They will leave the baseball speech on the cutting room floor, but you've got to do this movie."

I'm most proud of the work I've done that draws from small projects. By that I mean simple stories. And *Field of Dreams* qualifies as a small story and also a successful film. In that movie, we were talking about spirit and magic, and to cover that, Fenway was the ideal park.

Field of Dreams qualifies as

a small story and also a successful film.

In that movie, we were talking about

spirit and magic, and to cover that,

Fenway was the ideal park.

— JAMES EARL JONES

Bucky Dent

Bucky Dent hit forty homers in eleven big league seasons, including a Fenway fly ball that won the 1978 Yankees–Red Sox playoff game. He now coaches for the Texas Rangers.

I don't think they'll get over it

until they actually win a World Series.

— BUCKY DENT

Bucky Dent is congratulated by Roy White (6) after hitting his homer during a playoff game at Fenway in 1978.

I WAS WITH THE WHITE SOX THE FIRST TIME I CAME TO Fenway. Everybody had always talked about it. It's kind of like Yankee Stadium and Wrigley Field. You hear a lot about it, but when you actually walk out there and see the Wall, you realize what an impact it has on you as a player. It's a neat place. It was always a fun place to play, but as a visitor, it was always a scary place to play. A lead is never safe. I remember being up by six runs late in a game with the White Sox and we lost. You never knew what was

going to happen. It was the same thing when I was with the Cardinals, playing at Wrigley Field.

I hit the Wall a few times and hit a few home runs here. As a shortstop, it presented some unique situations. When I first came here, they made sure I knew that when a ball went down the line I had to come out, because it might come off that wall and kick back toward the infield.

When I went to bat in the playoff game, I was just trying to get a base hit. We were down two runs. I never thought about trying to hit a home run, it's just that here, if you get a ball inside, it's possible to hit a home run, to be able to jerk one out. In that situation, I got a pitch that I could pull, and I happened to hit it on a line. When I hit the ball, I didn't think it was going out. I didn't think it was high enough to get over the Wall. I thought it was going to hit the top of the Wall. When I hit it, I was trying to run from home plate to get to second. When I was rounding first, I saw the signal that it went out. I never saw it go over the Wall.

It's always special for me to come back here. It's just a good place to come and play. The crowd is on you, and you've got the Wall in left field, and the game is different every time. It's a lot of fun. I coached first base here one night with Texas, and they booed me.

It's always going to be there. I come to Boston a lot because I do some PR for a company in Auburn, Massachusetts. It's unbelievable. I met the guy that owns the company at a Yankee Fantasy Camp. We hit it off, and here I am twelve years later. I go back and forth every year to Boston. I come up to play golf or talk baseball with the customers. I enjoy it. It's fun to come back here. It's interesting because everybody knows where they were when I hit the home run. It's something because of the magnitude of the Red Sox history and the Yankee history, our catching them on the last day. There was so much riding on that game. It was a special day. One of those things that doesn't come along very often.

When I travel around in the Boston area, there isn't a day that goes by when I don't have somebody come up to me and tell me I broke their heart twenty years ago. Everybody kind of remembers that game and that day. I remember a couple of years ago I came up here to play some golf with some customers on Cape Cod. There was a bar out there and the bartender was a diehard Red Sox fan, and after the golf game they told me, "You've got to come over and see this guy. We're going to bring you in there, sit you down, and see if this guy recognizes you." It was the year of the strike, and he was such a big fan, he had all the baseball hats in his bar covered up because of the strike. So I walked in and sat down, and he looked at me and his face kind of dropped. I said, "Hi, I'm Bucky Dent," and he said, "I know who you are." It happens.

I don't think the people from my time will get over it. Some of the younger kids that don't know what that game was, eventually they'll forget about it. But the people that saw the game, or were here, or part of it, I don't think they'll get over it until they actually win a World Series, and then they can get rid of the old memories.

When people tell me they are Red Sox fans, I like to joke around with them and get them talking about that season. I remember that last at-bat of that playoff game. I remember standing at shortstop for the matchup between Gossage and Yastrzemski. I can still see Gossage throwing a fastball right down the middle that popped him up. Those things just don't go away.

That year was magical. It's a shame they didn't have a wild card then. You take New York and Boston and the history of the Red Sox and the Yankees and then it comes down to one day. I think that's what frustrates the Red Sox fans so much. There was just that one day, and then it didn't happen for them again. I hear about it around this time of year, every time the Red Sox are trying to make a run at winning the division or getting in the playoffs.

We have Little Fenway at my baseball school in Delray Beach, Florida. We were going to redo one field and we just felt it would be neat to do something different for the kids. A lot of the kids will never experience playing in Fenway, so putting up a normal field was nothing new. We wanted to give them a feel of playing in a ballpark with that kind of atmosphere, or a visualization of hitting one out. That's what we created. And over the years, the dads have really gotten a charge out of going out there and trying to hit one out. We tried to build it the same. The only difference is that this wall is 37 feet and ours is 34.

I'd hate to see them tear down Fenway. It's like Yankee Stadium. There's just certain parks that have that magical feeling when you walk in 'em. The new stadiums are nice, but there's just something magical about Yankee Stadium, Wrigley Field, and Fenway. They're special places, but you don't have that atmosphere anymore. I'd find a way to redo the stadium and keep that mystique of what it's all about.

When you're talking about Fenway, you're talking about The Game. The one game for me.

Bud Selig

Bud Selig is the commissioner of baseball.

CLUBS GET TIRED OF ME TALKING ABOUT HISTORY all the time, but you can't really love baseball without loving history. There are only two parks that I've loved from the time I was a kid to now. One would be Wrigley Field in Chicago and the other would be Fenway Park in Boston. There is a uniqueness. Fenway and Wrigley manifest the history of the game better than any other ballparks I know. All you have to do is walk in and you feel it and sense it.

In 1949, my mother and I were in New York. I was a great Yankee fan, a great Joe DiMaggio fan. We went up to

Boston, and my mother wanted to take me to art galleries and things like that. But she loved baseball and we went to Fenway Park. The Yankees were there. I was fifteen. We walked up to the ticket window. I'll never forget it. My mother told the man at the ticket window, "I've brought my boy from Milwaukee. We want to go to the game." He slammed the window and said, "Sorry, lady, we're sold out." My mother and I walked around Fenway for two hours trying to figure a way to get into the game. We never did.

The first time I went to Fenway was about three or four years later, when I was still in college. Even today, it's a tie to history. You just can't say that about any other ballpark. Yankee Stadium comes close, but Fenway is Fenway. You think of Ted Williams and of all the old Yankee–Red Sox games.

John Harrington is a close friend. Nobody loves the history of the game more than I do. But with everything I'm telling you about Fenway Park, the Red Sox can't survive without a new ballpark. We can talk about how it's regrettable and it's wrong that the economics have forced clubs to do this, but given where they are with Fenway, they just need a new stadium. And it'll break my heart, too. But on the other hand, the important thing is that the Red Sox continue to be viable. We found in Milwaukee that rebuilding the existing park just wasn't practical. It turned out to be far more expensive and very inefficient. There's no question that a little of you dies when you lose a park like that.

Doris Kearns Goodwin

Doris Kearns Goodwin is a Pulitzer Prize–winning author, a historian, and a Red Sox season ticket holder.

I FELL IN LOVE WITH FENWAY PARK BEFORE I FELL IN love with the Red Sox. I came to Boston in the fall of '64 for graduate school at Harvard, but I didn't go to Fenway until the next summer. The first time I went to Fenway Park was actually the first time I'd been to a baseball game since the Dodgers left Brooklyn [1957]. I just lost any caring about baseball once the Dodgers left Brooklyn. My father had made the transition to the Mets,

but I couldn't make any transition. So really, baseball had left my life. It was partly also my age, I suppose. It was during that time when I graduated from high school and then college. But somehow, that very first time I went to Fenway Park—a boyfriend took me and it was a beautiful summer night, probably in June—and somehow all the memories of Ebbetts Field came back. It was the same kind of park, small and overcrowded, and there were lots of people there even though the Red Sox weren't doing well then. All the peculiar characteristics of the park brought back memories of Ebbetts Field. Probably most important, the fans were so close to the field—yelling and screaming and knowing what was going on—and that was so reminiscent of the Brooklyn Dodgers. So my return to baseball, and the beginning of what has now been another three decades of obsession, started with that first night at Fenway Park.

I know where I sat that night, and it's still my favorite place. We somehow had lower box seats between home and first. Later, when my husband and I got our first season tickets in 1976, they were in that same area. Now we've been upgraded to the area below the walkway aisle, but we're between home and third base, and I don't feel the same familiarity. I still miss that other place.

We started taking our boys when they were about three or four. We didn't stay for the whole game. They loved to go for the hot dogs and all the food. We gradually worked them into it, and by '86 they were full-fledged fans. The fact that it was small meant that they felt a mastery of it even as little kids. I can still remember that feeling when you walk down the ramp when you first come in and turn right, and they knew exactly where to run to go to our seats. I suppose you could learn that in a big Astrodome, but not with the same sense of comfort. When they got a little older, I felt comfortable letting them go to get a snack by themselves. You knew they'd find their way back. And there was a wonderful guy in the information booth. Al. He's a terrific fellow. He's been there forever. He used to be an usher and we only had three seats in '86, and he let Joey, who was only nine, sneak in and sit on our laps during the World Series. There was a specialness in that for the boys. They would come in and high-five him. Even now they go to talk to him, and I think that creates part of the familiarity of a small park and the people who've been there for a long time that I don't think would be the same in a larger place.

Fenway becomes like a piece of furniture in your household. It's as if you've got a couch that may be a little bit old and torn in places, but it's comfortable and familiar, and it's got a lot of memories. I don't care about the bathrooms the way they are. I don't care about having more comfortable seats. But the only thing I do understand is that if it's necessary to make the team competitive and win a World Series—and having now seen the new stadiums in Baltimore and Colorado, and feeling less worried that we'd go into a big dome with no character—I would not be out on the picket line to save Fenway. I would have done that had I not seen those other stadiums. But other than for the club to have more revenue, which benefits all of us, I don't see any need to change Fenway Park. And my husband points out that Fenway hasn't exactly been a good luck charm.

If they tear it down, I'll probably feel pretty terrible. Nothing can feel the same as the last time I went to Ebbets Field. But at least this time I'll know that I'll still be attending games over at the new place. But memories do get attached to a place. There's no question about that. I can still remember the first game of the 1986 World Series, and all the people we saw at the park before the game and the excitement and the buzz in the crowd. My greatest desire is to come out of the final game of a World Series that we won and picturing Yawkey Way. There's a real physical feeling of imagining what it might be like, having the ballpark on your right and picturing those vendors out there. To think that that might never happen is really sad and tough to imagine. I think there's no question that it will take away that whole cascade of memories once the park is gone.

Fenway becomes like a piece

of furniture in your household.

It's as if you've got a couch that may

be a little bit old and torn in places, but

it's comfortable and familiar,

and it's got a lot of old memories.

— DORIS KEARNS GOODWIN

Nomar Garciaparra wears a 1908 Red Sox uniform in an interleague game against the Atlanta Braves in 1997.

Carl Yastrzemski

Carl Yastrzemski played for the Red Sox from 1961 to 1983 and
was inducted into the Hall of Fame in 1989.

I FIRST VISITED FENWAY IN 1959 WHEN I SIGNED.
We went around to all the different teams I was interested in signing with. I did a Thanksgiving vacation tour
my freshman year at Notre Dame when I made up my
mind to sign. I stopped at Cincinnati first, then Detroit,
then Fenway. Cincinnati had Crosley Field, which was a
great ballpark to hit in, and Detroit's a great ballpark to
hit in. I walked into Fenway and it was snowing. And I'm
standing up by the executive offices overlooking the field
with my dad. Somebody said, "Boy, this is a good ballpark
to hit in," and I looked and said, "Jesus Christ, you can't
even see right field, it's so far away." And after coming
from Detroit and Crosley Field, it did look far. To tell you
the truth, I was more interested in going either with the
Yankees or Cincinnati or Detroit because of the ballparks.
But my dad had a priest friend on Long Island, Father Joe.
And he kept saying, "You have to play for Mr. Yawkey." At
that time, my dad had to cosign the contract, so that's
how I ended up with the Red Sox.

I think Fenway's a great ballpark for the fans. The
new one, they keep talking about it, but I don't see
anything happening. So I don't even worry about it. I
think Fenway's great and they should keep it, but maybe
for financial reasons they have to come up with a new
ballpark. I like these new ballparks in Cleveland and
Baltimore. They're good hitters' ballparks and you got
a lot of action and the fans are close. I hated those symmetrical ballparks.

I think the closeness of the seats in Fenway is what I
liked the best. You'd come off a road trip where you
played in Cleveland or Oakland, like you were in some
coliseum where the fans weren't into it and it was hard for
you to get into it. But as soon as you stepped onto the
field at Fenway Park, you got into it real quick because of
the closeness of those seats.

I've always said, you can't hide in it. If you have a
horseshit day, everybody sees it at the ballpark and writes
about it in the papers. People see it on TV. Why cover it
up? Just admit to it. It's that simple. You're human. I inter-
acted with the fans a little bit between innings. I think by
doing it, you would win 'em over on your side, instead of
ignoring them. The scoreboard guys kept me informed.
They had a couple of kids out there. Joe Mooney's ground
crew. Joe would throw them in there as punishment, I
think.

When I first got to Boston, the Wall was cement and
then tin. Then they went with the plastic or whatever they
call it now. When they put that in, back in the late '70s, it
was easier to play the Wall. Before, when you had the tin
and the rivets, and those two-by-fours every few feet, you
never knew where the ball was going to come off. If it hit
the two-by-fours, the ball would bounce back just as if it
had hit the cement. If it hit the dead spot, it would just
drop down. Then it might rattle around the ladder and
you'd just have to wait for it to come down. There was
nothing you could do. It made it interesting playing there.
But I loved having that thing behind me. I can remember
Frank Howard coming into Fenway Park and I'd play him
right behind shortstop. And I'd play between short and
third base, trying to take away the line drive base hit.
Or make a play on him at first base. Playing left field at
Fenway, you took a position where you don't have so
much action and made it into a place where you had a lot
of action. Decoying. Stuff like that. The pitchers used to
get pissed off if I didn't move on a home run. They'd say,
"Jesus Christ, at least make an attempt to go back." But I
was setting it up for a case when if a guy hit a ball that I
knew was going to go off the Wall, I'd stand there like I
knew it was going to be a home run, and maybe he'd start
trotting to first and we could hold him to a single. So
there was a method to doing all that. When they take the
Wall down and move into a new park, I want to get a little
piece of it.

I loved Fenway. I just loved it there. I knew everybody
by their name. I knew all the concessions people, and I'd
stop in there before the games. When you came to the
ballpark, to me it was like being at home. It was like just
going to your home.

Let me get this straight: We're bulldozing real vintage ballparks

like Tiger Stadium and Fenway Park to put up fake vintage ballparks?

—RICK REILLY, *SPORTS ILLUSTRATED*

I loved Fenway.

When you came to the ballpark,

to me it was like being at home.

It was just like going to your home.

— CARL YASTRZEMSKI

acknowledgments   The authors would like to thank Ted Williams, Buzz Hamon, Lee Serra, Judy Bailey, John Henry Williams, Dick Johnson, Kevin Shea, Kate Gordon, Tim Samway, Dan Casey, Matt Storin, Ben Taylor, Ben Bradlee Jr., Don Skwar, Kate Shaughnessy, Stephen Stills, Steve Sheppard, Robin Young, Renee Masi, Lesley Visser, Meg Blackstone, Mike Barnicle, Ed Kleven, Kevin Dupont, Peter Gammons, Dave Smith, Bill Tanton, Vince Doria, Tim Kurkjian, Laurel Prieb, Wendy Selig-Prieb, Phyllis Merhige, Joe Sullivan, Will McDonough, Guy Spina, Bob Lobel, Bob Levin, Glenn Stout, John Iannacci, John Horn, Eric Monroe, Dick Bresciani, Helen Robinson, Mary Jane Ryan, Debbie Matson, Tom Mulvoy, Sean Mullin, Jonny Miller, Mike McHugh, Gordon Edes, Jeff Idelson, Sue Callaghan, and all those who agreed to be interviewed.

Thanks to the Hood blimp, Paul Comerford, the Squantum Seven, Mayor Thomas Menino, Lynne Smith, Deborah Wrobleski, Steve Shaughnessy, Shaughnessy Aerialifts, Jim Davis, Brian Kaplan, Mary Beth Kabat, Jean Shiner, Erica Pearl, Samantha Palmer, Peter Southwick, the *Globe*'s Photo Department, Vincent Musi, Callie Shell, Wil Haygood, Tim Dwyer, David Nyhan, Julia Talcott, Mike LaVigne, Michael Sturgis, Catie Aldrich, Nikon Professional Services, Zona Color Lab in Cambridge, and the New England Sports Museum.

Special thanks to Gary Smith for believing in the project and to Marnie Cochran, Luise Erdmann, Wendy Strothman, and Chris Coffin at Houghton Mifflin. And to Joe Mooney. Thanks to Bill Marr and Sarah Leen, Legal Sea Foods, and to Arthur D'Angelo of Twins Enterprises.

As always, a big thanks to our families. Dan appreciates the help and patience of Marilou, Sarah, Kate, and Sam. Stan would like to thank his wife, Stacey Kabat, for being a temporary baseball widow, his son Samuel, his dad Purroy, his mother Mildred, his sister Sandy, and Howie and Bert Bauer, who got him tickets to the 1967 World Series.